PRAISE FC

"This book, in its focus on wholeness, is a clear and compelling answer to the fragmented life we lead and the fragmented world around us. Wendy provides the images, the stories and a practical path to the integration of Eastern values and Western thinking that is both good for the soul and good for our organisations."

PETER BLOCK

Author of *Flawless Consulting* and *Stewardship*

"Wendy's wonderful book is a compelling reminder to live in the present, aware and awake. As the pace and intensity of modern life ratchet up, her emphasis on wholeness is more important than ever."

MARSHALL GOLDSMITH

Executive coach, business educator,
New York Times bestselling author, and
#1 leadership thinker in the world (Thinkers50 ranking)

"Wendy's invitation into wholeness brings to mind another phrase, 'living completely', the idea of embracing life and its challenges while leaving behind what drains us. Filled with thoughtful examples, Wendy guides leaders and professionals on a path to show how work and family can provide meaning and harmony to one's life, whilst contributing to the larger good."

MAYA HU-CHAN

President, Global Leadership Associates and
co-author of *Global Leadership: The Next Generation*

"While much of the leadership literature focuses on doing and leading others, Wendy provides an existentialist perspective of the leaders' personal inner journey towards Wholeness and Being. I read with joy that leadership is a journey of awakening – uncovering, unfolding and reclaiming the very gifts that have been all along within us. In this journey we become Wisdom, Peace and Grace. A great read and encouragement for leaders embarking on this journey of awakening."

Dr LIM BOON HUAT
Managing Director, Rohde & Schwarz

"Drawing on her Eastern heritage and Western education, Wendy's unique voice and message on individual and community wholeness are timely. The stories in the book paint a possibility of dealing with workplace realities while becoming our better selves."

TERRI EGAN, PhD
Associate Professor of Applied Behavioural Science,
Graziadio School of Management and Business,
Pepperdine University

"Wendy's book offers a refreshing perspective on how being whole as an individual is both a precursor and result of being whole as a community. We are not complete as people until we have connected with others around us. This can be as simple as noticing a stranger, sharing a smile, offering service to others or most importantly, by being simply present to one another. Through honouring one another, we transform the experience of being with one another into a broader experience of wholeness, connectedness and meaning."

MELISSA ARATANI KWEE
CEO, National Volunteer and Philanthropic Centre

"This book speaks to the magic of remembering what's important. Wendy's writing on Wholeness is a gift because it's not about being perfect or having all the answers. Rather, it strengthens our readiness to just be and to find a way to go towards what makes us, our families and our teams special."

ANDREW MATTHEWS

Chief Actuary, Medibank Private

"Fluent in the ways of the West and the East, Wendy tells through these stories a journey towards wholeness in individuals and organisations. Thirdness as a fusion of the parts is a creative idea to contemplate. Recommended for leaders who want meaning and success."

BEVERLY KAYE

Co-author of *Love 'Em or Lose 'Em* and *Help Them Grow or Watch Them Go*

"The Chinese believe the world is made of *yin* and *yang*. This book gives real-life examples of how different kinds of *yin* and *yang* come together in our life and at work to make a difference. The most intriguing *yin-yang* interactions definitely come from the different Eastern and Western cultural practices depicted in this book. Very insightful!"

Dr DAVID CHANG

Vice President, Roche Pharma Technical Operations, China

"Wendy shares her life-threatening experience that evolved into wholeness. She shares her passion to enrich other people's lives as hers has been from finding that rare balance and tranquillity in a hectic life. Take a moment, pause and reflect and feel the difference as you turn each page."

ROBIN SPECULAND

Global pioneer and expert in strategy implementation

"In touch with the work dilemmas facing the current generation, this book articulates a cohesive approach to life and leadership. It holds out hope for all of us to become our better selves and the possibility for community at the workplace. An excellent book for leaders more intent on changing themselves than changing others."

GEOFF BELLMAN

Author of *The Consultant's Calling* and *Extraordinary Groups*

"Wendy's book is a refreshing reminder to organisations, leaders and individuals on what it takes to thrive in a fast-changing and increasingly inter-connected world – not to focus on parts but the wholeness from interconnected relationships."

LAU YIN CHENG

Advisor to C-level executives and formerly Chief of HR & OD, Infocomm Development Authority of Singapore

"Like many books on leadership and personal mastery, Wendy shares some fascinating concepts and ideas, centred on the idea of wholeness and congruence. Unlike many other books, she also devotes much time to the actions, big and small, that we can take to make these ideas live and breathe. Anyone who cares about being a better person and leader will benefit from her wisdom and insight."

AARON MANIAM

Poet and civil servant

"In a fresh and vital new voice, Wendy enchantingly leads us to integrate Western and Eastern wisdom to create the world we wish for ourselves, our families, and our organisations. If you are weary of fragmentation and disconnection, reading and practising the tools in this book can help you regain your wholeness."

PAULINE ARNEBERG, PhD

Faculty, Masters of Public Administration, California State University Northridge

wholeness in a disruptive world

PEARLS OF WISDOM FROM EAST AND WEST

WENDY TAN

Dear Dhanesh,

So glad we stayed connected all these years! Wishing you wholeness in your work/life!

Warmly,
Wendy 2018

Marshall Cavendish Business

Published in 2017 by Marshall Cavendish Business
An imprint of Marshall Cavendish International

A member of the
Times Publishing Group

Other Marshall Cavendish Offices:
Marshall Cavendish Corporation. 99 White Plains Road, Tarrytown NY 10591-9001, USA • Marshall Cavendish International (Thailand) Co Ltd. 253 Asoke, 12th Flr, Sukhumvit 21 Road, Klongtoey Nua, Wattana, Bangkok 10110, Thailand • Marshall Cavendish (Malaysia) Sdn Bhd, Times Subang, Lot 46, Subang Hi-Tech Industrial Park, Batu Tiga, 40000 Shah Alam, Selangor Darul Ehsan, Malaysia

National Library Board, Singapore Cataloguing-in-Publication Data
Names: Tan, Wendy.
Title: Wholeness in a Disruptive World : Pearls of wisdom from East and West / Wendy Tan.
Description: Singapore : Marshall Cavendish Business, 2017.
Identifiers: OCN 974772036 | 978-981-4771-90-0 (paperback)
Subjects: LCSH: Management. | Leadership. | Organizational change | Self-actualization (Psychology)
Classification: DDC 650.13--dc23

Printed in Singapore by Markono Print Media Pte Ltd

To Pete, Finn, Sophie and Kang Yam –
thank you for making my life whole

CONTENTS

wholeness

noun

1. Individual wholeness: a sense of completeness and balance within oneself and with the community.
2. Collective wholeness: the well-being of the larger whole – family, team, organisation and community.
3. Cognitive wholeness: balancing opposites in our thinking.
4. Parts coming together to create something more expansive and life-giving – thirdness.
5. Not just a state but also a process of continuous balancing and rebalancing.

disruptive world

noun

1. Fast-changing business model that transforms the way the industry delivers value.
2. Uncertain, ambiguous, complex and potentially stressful landscape to navigate.
3. Requires organisations and people to respond in new ways.

WELCOME
WHY I WROTE THIS BOOK

Lying in the hospital's intensive care unit for four days, I drifted in and out of consciousness. Amid the busy hum of nurses and doctors making their rounds, concerned check-ins, and the constant beeping of the resuscitation equipment, I found myself wondering, "Is this the end?"

My three young children, Pete, Finn and Sophie, came to mind. I felt deeply regretful. Perhaps I would not see them grow up. I would not help Pete transition into primary school or cheer for him in his swim competitions. I would not read to Finn or laugh at his adorable pouting. I would miss seeing Sophie, a tomboy, dolled up in dresses. I could not bear the thought of not seeing them grow up. What would they be like in the terrible teenage years and as hopefully responsible adults? Leaning over weakly on the hospital bed, I choked at my request to my parents and godmother to take care of the three kids.

As an achievement-oriented and hyper-efficient professional and mother, I had lived my life constantly ticking off items on my "to do" list (only to have more the next day). I organised my life in blocks of 15 minutes. I struggled to do it all – deliver good work, manage my business and be a good mother. My time, energy and attention were fragmenting. My life was fragmenting.

While I lay on that hospital bed, I could see that it wasn't only me. My frenzied pace – with fragmented attention, energy and way of being – was a mirror of our larger world today. More than ever before, the pace quickens with 24/7 connection to our gadgets. Competition stiffens with lower-cost labour from elsewhere. Threats heighten as technology disrupts business models. Job security dips to new lows with increasing use of automation and artificial intelligence. Challenges mount as new skills are needed to survive in the changing landscape. None of these make us whole.

Thankfully, in the course of the week that felt like an eternity, the strongest antibiotics gradually helped my body gain the upper hand. My vital statistics returned to normalcy gradually. Discharged on New Year's Eve, I was relieved to be home. My life had been saved, but my energy was sapped. From zipping to and from locations or tasks in blocks of 15 minutes, I could only catch my next breath and pause. Without vitality, I stopped work and travel for more than a year.

To regain my health, I picked up *taiji* and *qigong*, and in the process got reacquainted with my Eastern roots. I saw that I had to find a different way of being. I still wanted to do good work, be a good mum and make my life count. Rushing around faster trying to "do it all" was just not sustainable. A question rang in my head: "What is the alternative to the fragmentation I experienced?"

Perhaps the Eastern perspective, with 5,000 years of history, would have something to offer. With its roots in the *Dao De Jing*, Confucianism and *yin-yang*, Eastern thinking *integrates* rather than *separates*. It focuses on the whole rather than individual parts. I contrasted it to my largely Western-based education in Singapore and the United States. A hallmark of Western management is to isolate and manage the *parts*.

It dawned on me that perhaps we can respond to this fragmentation with a new way of thinking – the integration of Eastern

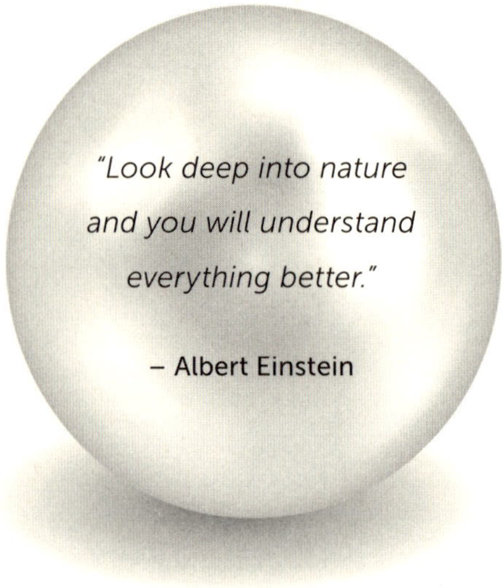

and Western thought. Pearls are formed at the intersection of land and sea. Imagine for a moment that the West is the land and the East is the sea. In the merging of ideologies between East and West, what are the pearls? How might these help us integrate work and life in a sustainable whole?

To answer these questions, I talked to leaders and executives who seemed to be at ease in both Eastern and Western worlds. They helped me understand how to stay whole and balanced in spite of the conundrums, conflicts and challenges we face in today's disruptive world. I researched how individuals and organisations can be healthy and deliver good work. Wholeness came as an alternative to this fragmentation. Wholeness is a sense of completeness and balance within oneself and with one's community.

OVERVIEW OF THE BOOK

This book brings together the pearls of both East and West so that you can be, think and act whole, and live your life and do your best work in the world. As Einstein said, "We cannot solve our problems with the same thinking we used when we created them."

This book explores the why, what and how of having more wholeness at work and in your life. It is written for professionals and leaders searching for greater alignment and harmony in today's fragmented world. If you have picked up this book, you probably identify with the experience of fragmentation, dilemma, and tension when leading yourself and others. Experiencing wholeness during holidays or in meditation retreats is good but insufficient. With challenges in everyday life, the quest is to be whole despite the tension we experience. My goal is to point to an alternative way of being, thinking and behaving that will allow you to be more whole – for yourself as well as for the greater good.

This book is also a cross-cultural book, relevant for executives and leaders who straddle the worlds of East and West and want to better understand the nuances of or resolve the conflicts arising in East-West interactions in business life. Thus, it is highly relevant reading for coaches and leadership development facilitators as well as people in the human development industry.

What will you discover in this book? Here is an overview:

Chapter 1: When Wholeness Is Missing

In this first chapter, you'll read about real-life examples of the lack of wholeness in individuals, teams and organisations that culminate in negative consequences at work and in life. This chapter guides you to reflect on what drains you and keeps wholeness elusive in your life.

Chapter 2: The Joys of Wholeness

Included in this chapter are stories of professionals, leaders and business owners who share their journeys toward wholeness. These stories give us clues on the pathway towards wholeness, highlighting the nourishment and wisdom that wholeness offers. You're encouraged to reflect on moments of wholeness in your own life.

Chapter 3: How Wholeness Works

"Wholeness" is one of those words that everyone seems to know the meaning of but no one has the same definition. This chapter pulls together ideas about what wholeness means. You'll think about what wholeness means to you personally.

Chapter 4: Anchoring

Anchoring is the first of the ABCs of wholeness. Anchors keep us rooted. Your anchor is who you are as an individual and who you are in relation to your community. Awareness of your anchor gives you clarity, courage and commitment. The deeper

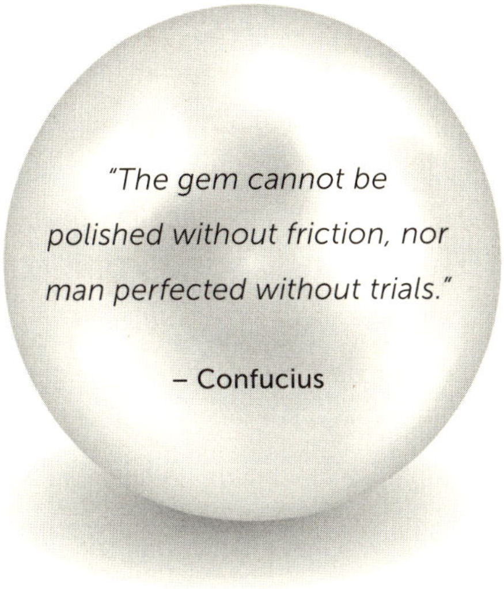

and wider your anchor, the more positive your impact. In this chapter, I invite you to clarify the dimensions of your anchor.

Chapter 5: Balancing

Is balance like a scale – when one side is up, the other side is necessarily down? Or is balance a 50:50 split, like a compromise? This chapter argues for dynamic balance being 100:100 over time, creating a *thirdness* that is more expansive and creative. You'll find 100:100 answers to any dilemma using the Mobius Insight™ Tool.

Chapter 6: Clearing

Clearing is about emptying yourself so that you can purposefully *be*. We are useful when we are empty – empty of judgments, ego and mental clutter. You increase your capacity to reflect in the moment, to be aware of your impact on your environment and to sense what's needed in any situation. This helps you act in wisdom. You are encouraged to experience an activity to empty out.

Chapter 7: Integrating the ABCs in a Disruptive World

This chapter integrates Anchoring, Balance and Clearing in the disruptive world that we live in today. You will think about how you can use these ABCs in your life and at work.

Epilogue: Wholeness Beyond "I"

Ultimately, wholeness is the larger community – your family, team, organisation, community or even the world at large. The sense of community refers to our capacity to be contributors rather than consumers, to care for strangers and to take responsibility for our impact on the world.

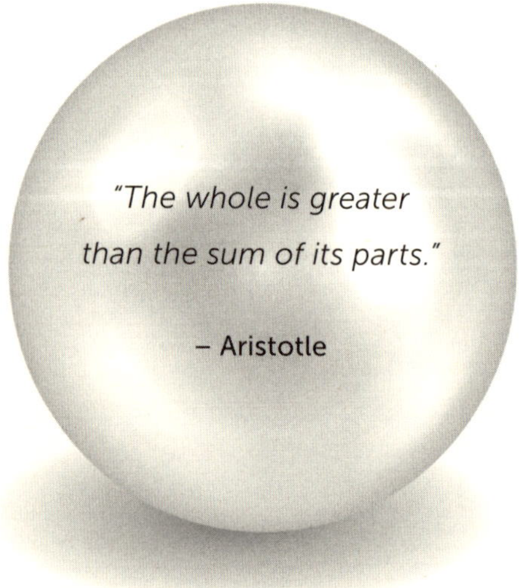

At the end of every chapter is an applied section, "Over to You", where you'll discover tools and exercises that will help you apply wholeness in your own work and life. Use these tools to generate new perspectives and responses to your existing questions. You can also refer to www.wholenessinadisruptiveworld.com for additional resources. I invite you to treat this book as a companion for reflection. There's no need to rush to the end of the book. Talk to friends about your thoughts and what ideas you might try. Better still, create your own wholeness community and support one another on your individual journeys.

As I reflect on my own life six years after my illness, I am grateful for these lessons. Today, I enjoy being with my children, appreciate simple meals with my family, challenge myself to contribute through my work, find fulfilment in making a difference in people's lives, and take time to listen to the wisdom of nature. I sincerely hope these ideas will be of service to you as you live your own life of wholeness.

PART I

THE MEANING OF WHOLENESS

WHOLENESS IS ONE OF THOSE WORDS which everyone knows the meaning of, but which is hard to express in words. I define wholeness as a sense of peace and being complete within oneself and with the world around. This sense of wholeness is dynamic and experienced in the moment. Wholeness is the "thirdness" created from the integration of polarities over time. When we are whole with our communities, we are authentic, adaptive and abundant.

In exploring this topic, I first look at situations where wholeness is missing. Lack of wholeness over time impacts one's productivity, physical and emotional health and capacity to contribute, ultimately to the detriment of the community around us. I also learn from leaders and professionals who seem whole despite the challenges they face – what does wholeness mean to them and what helps them be whole? These individuals have a different way of being and thinking, an ability to embrace polarities and act in context.

Learning from these stories and drawing insights from East/West thinking, I explore the what and why of wholeness in the following chapters. This notion of wholeness is different from therapy or the religious sense of wholeness; it is a wholeness that acknowledges all the realities of the modern world and embraces the role of work in our lives.

CHAPTER 1
WHEN WHOLENESS IS MISSING

"Mastery does not mean having a plan for the whole, but having an awareness of the whole."
– Peter Senge, *The Dance of Change*

Consider these scenarios:

- A leader, caught in the ceaseless scurry of activities, runs even faster knowing that impending organisation changes will bring about even more work. He knows he needs to shift his focus to longer-term strategic priorities given the rapidly changing environment; however, he feels depleted by today's demands.

- A site director wants to build a high-performing organisation where people innovate for the future. But preoccupied by business challenges, she unknowingly distances herself from her people. Spending long hours at work, she finds there's little to talk about at home with her family beyond the functional necessities.

- A smart, ambitious finance director is in line to succeed the managing director, but struggles to be a career woman and a mother to her two young sons. Feeling conflicted, she quits.

- A Chinese leader with impeccable technical skills is now the only Asian among a group of Westerners in the top leadership team. He realises he needs to make his presence known by making a "show", but he hesitates – he has always "led from the back".

- An American leader, posted to Shanghai for the first time, feels the pressure to show results and tries to drive change by defining strategies, KPIs and reward systems. His people respond with a verbal "yes" but nothing changes. He takes it personally and becomes more aggressive.

- Despite feeling stagnant at work, a manager doesn't leave his job because his family depends on him to provide for them financially. Being practical and responsible, he stays on but wonders if he needs to take some risks and venture into new areas to remain relevant in the digital age.

- A young professional with great potential lands a plum role – good career prospects, comfortable paycheck and big title – but yearns for the adventure of being his own boss and creating his own products.

These are composite examples drawn from the stories of professionals and leaders I have interacted with. Was there a scenario that resonated with you? If so, which one, and why?

These are examples of lives in which wholeness is missing. When this happens, we can still function in our lives and even be successful by external standards. But we may not feel happy or fulfilled. The lack of wholeness comes from:

- A conflict between who we are being and our true self

- Fragmentation in our attention, focus and energy

- Artificial compartmentalisation in our thinking
- Losing sight of what's truly important

This fragmentation creates a variety of unwelcome feelings. A manager describes it as being spun around in a washing machine by external forces and losing one's sense of control. You may also find yourself describing the feeling as:

- Lost
- Confused
- Conflicted
- Dissatisfied
- Burdened
- Uncertain
- Incomplete

Let's dive into the worlds of a few people and examine the factors that led to their circumstances. These stories are based on real people I have met at work.

> *"When the wind of change blows, some build walls and others build windmills."*
>
> **– Chinese proverb**

Alan – Cares but exhausted

Staring out of the window from his workstation, Alan ponders, "Fifteen percent year-on-year improvement..." A manufacturing site director, Alan faces relentless pressure to lower the production cost of goods. Meeting all targets in one fiscal year results in even higher targets the following year. Meeting the challenge of beating those key performance indicators (KPIs) risks dissipating the creativity that makes it happen.

Looking at his calendar on the computer, many thoughts bombard his mind. "Operational meeting at 3 p.m., quarterly strategic review, Edwin's request, change in attitude in Lian, survey results, boss visit in two weeks..." His train of thought is interrupted by an urgent email arriving in his inbox. He clicks on it.

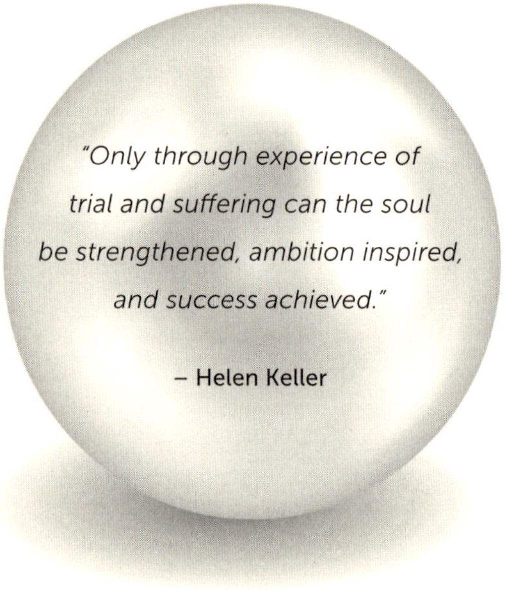

"Only through experience of trial and suffering can the soul be strengthened, ambition inspired, and success achieved."

– Helen Keller

Alan's routine, on top of frequent travel in the region, is both gruelling and draining. He is caught in an endless flurry of activities, a race without a finish line. Knowing that impending organisational changes will mean more work and uncertainty, he runs even faster. He needs to shift his focus to long-term strategic priorities. The waves of technology changes could impact or even erode their competitive advantage. However, he is depleted by today's demands.

Alan genuinely cares for his team. He wants to build a workplace where the employees learn and grow together. He knows he has good people, but all isn't rosy. The employee opinion survey shows only 40 percent are "emotionally and mentally engaged", one-third "disengaging and open to other opportunities" and the rest "on the fence".

A recent integration announcement signals change and uncertainty for the short term, compounding employee stressors. Some employees are worried about keeping their jobs as an automation project moves forward. Many employees put in long hours on the job, and including the long commute, they spend 12 to 14 hours on work. Two high-potential executives recently resigned, citing "family reasons". But we know that's a diplomatic way to say quits.

Alan gets home at 8 p.m., a typical time for him. His family members have already eaten. Fatigued but still preoccupied with work, he asks his two children in passing, "Have you done your homework? Anything to sign?" They answer in monosyllables without raising their heads from their gadgets.

"There's a late-night teleconference with the global team tonight," thinks Alan, as he eats his late dinner alone. After the meeting, he finishes some paperwork and goes to sleep at 1 a.m., exhausted but at peace that he has checked off most of the items on his list. A similar routine repeats the next day.

What is happening in Alan's situation? His situation is typical of many modern-day executives as organisations continually restructure, resize and restrategise to survive. Studies show that 41 percent of organisations either recently completed a significant transformation initiative or are currently undergoing one. Another 47 percent are preparing to do so.[1]

The average lifespan of a company listed in the Standard & Poor's 500 Index of leading U.S. companies has decreased by more than 50 years over the last century – from 67 years in the 1920s to only 15 years today.[2] Planning horizons are shorter, strategy implementation has less lead time and people are repeatedly asked to do more with less. In addition, a Tower Watson worldwide survey shows that 50 percent of employees say their workload has increased in the past three years.[3] Eighty-three percent of American employees are stressed by at least one thing at work, especially workload and pay, up from 73 percent in 2012.[4]

In our globalised environment, many people operate across multiple time zones. Conflicts between work and personal lives deepen as conference calls take place in the late evening or early morning hours. Additionally, we find it hard to switch off from our gadgets – 80 percent of smartphone users check their phones first thing in the morning[5].

Alan is worn out from this treadmill mode, which doesn't give him time or space to reflect on long-term or strategic issues. Despite his good intentions about creating a workplace in which people thrive, his subordinates are also experiencing the stress, and some are opting out physically or mentally. In addition, Alan feels emotionally disconnected from his family, which further reduces his support.

These issues accumulate, contributing to a sense of meaninglessness. What happens if Alan continues this cycle? Burnout, not to mention suboptimal performance, are often the consequences. He also misses the opportunity to connect meaningfully with his colleagues and family.

Let's meet another professional, who's facing a different challenge:

Maggie – Successful but conflicted

Maggie, a smart and achievement-oriented manager, is expected to succeed as the managing director in a few years. She will be the first woman to helm the organisation. Strategic-thinking, assertive and yet gracious, she has been mentored by the current managing director and is well respected by the employees.

One morning, Maggie comes to work with puffy red eyes. She thinks, "I can't do this anymore. Laura needs me." Maggie has two children, Edwin and Laura, who are seven and four years old, respectively. She has been struggling to balance work and family demands for a while. She has managed to avoid travel that would take her far from home by sending her managers with the intention of developing them too. She has also tried

> *"When we are not whole, our inner light cannot illuminate the work we do in the world."*
>
> **– Parker Palmer**

working at home on two afternoons each week, and when she's at the office, she leaves promptly at the end of the workday. "I am doing everything I can, but it's still not enough!" she laments.

The previous night, Edwin complained, "Mummy, why does Carol's mother help him with his homework in the afternoons but we always have to do it at night? I am tired at night." This morning, Laura wailed when Maggie dropped her off at pre-school, screaming, "Mummy, Mummy, don't leave me here! I want you to be with me!"

Maggie feels conflicted. She wants to spend her best energy with her children and has considered resigning many times. Her heart is with the kids, yet she doesn't feel like she's a "good mum" to them. Her mind, however, focuses on the pragmatics of living expenses and giving the best to the children. Her professional role is also part of how she sees herself and she doesn't relish the thought of giving up her career, her income – and her identity.

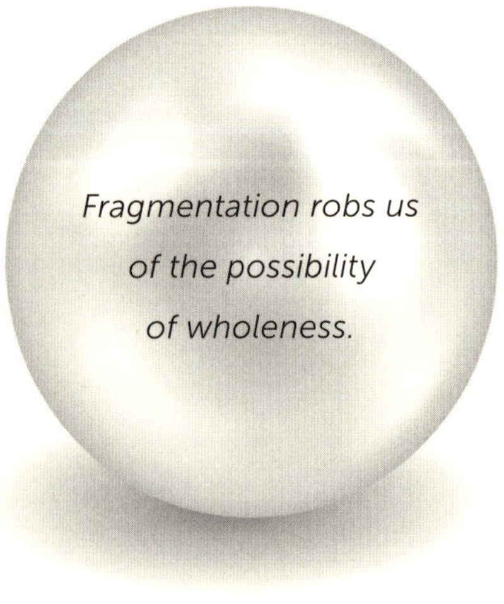

According to the American Psychological Association[6], Maggie is one of the 55 percent of employees who say that job demands have interfered with responsibilities at home. On the home front, it's increasingly challenging to raise a family and have a thriving career, especially with dual-income families. In a hyper-competitive world, we often worry about our children's future. From a young age, we expect them to perform well in academics, sports and music. Then we throw in expectations such as manners, values and cultural sensitivity. What happens? Full-blown performance management at home. On top of parenting, many also have the load of taking care of their elderly parents, as life expectancy increases.

Choosing either personal life or career is not a holistic solution. Not only is it a less-than-optimal choice for Maggie personally, there are also missed opportunities for the organisation to lose its talent. Why should the decision be *either* family or work anyway? Why not *both* family and work? Perhaps a different way of thinking can help us find creative new solutions rather than be trapped in unfulfilling compromises?

Let's meet our last example:

Dave and Liza – Culture clash

Relieved to be out of the sardine-packed subway and striding towards his office skyscraper in downtown Shanghai, Dave thinks to himself, "I don't understand why they can't just get it done. It's so straightforward! They are probably playing games here!"

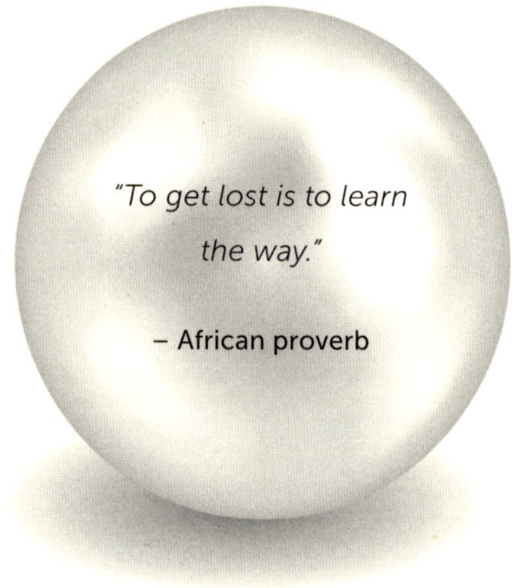

"To get lost is to learn the way."

– African proverb

Dave is an integration manager from America. His company, a Fortune 500 company, has acquired a software engineering company in China. Integration efforts have been ongoing for some time without significant progress. On paper, the harmonisation on job titles, organisation structure, headcounts, reporting lines, systems and processes is ready.

But he is frustrated by the speed of transition. He's under pressure to deliver savings on this acquisition, which will, in part, come from downsizing and eliminating duplicate resources. The local management team in China has verbally agreed to the changes, but the implementation has been much delayed. He has told Liza, the HR director, to go ahead with the redundancy plans.

Liza, a Taiwanese-born Chinese, earned her MBA in the United States and worked there for a few years before moving to

China. She understands how work in Western culture is seen as professional (which really means "don't get too personal") and plans are implemented in a logical and structured manner. At the same time, she knows that retrenching people on short notice goes against the implicit contract between the management and the employees. Requiring existing staff to re-apply for their jobs does not give the employees "face" or recognition for their years of experience and contribution. So although from a Western impersonal business perspective these processes are fair and efficient, they can also destroy the relationship and loyalty in the process. She wonders how she can bridge the gap in understanding.

This example is about the clash between Eastern and Western cultures in organisations. Just as a typical three-course Western meal usually proceeds in a step-by-step manner (starter, main dish, dessert or coffee), so does Western management thought. Leaders define strategy, key performance indicators are set, departments receive priorities, employees develop work plans, and we measure obsessively. Balanced scorecard, management by objectives, and business process re-engineering form the backbone of modern organisations. The output is systematic structure and processes to achieve results efficiently. These enable continuous improvement and have paved the way for the development of the present multinational mega-corporations.

Employees are also expected to be professionals, and relationships are transactions governed by contract – an exchange of time and expertise for money. Westerners prefer clarity in black-and-white terms and are less comfortable with ambiguity.

Driven by quarterly results, Westerners also favour quick actions with overnight results. At the same time, this mechanistic and reductionist approach assumes control and predictability over outcome. In Dave's example, he uses a logical and step-by-step approach to control the outcome.

However, the Chinese way differs. In a typical Chinese meal at home, all the dishes are placed in the middle. People are given a bowl of rice, and from the dishes in the middle they take what they want, in the amount they want, when they want it. In contrast to sequential dishes in three-course Western meals, the absence of a systematic process gives space for flexibility and emergent responses. Chinese thinking is flexible and emergent, rather than linear and logic-based. The Chinese phrase 摸石头过河 (*mo shi tou guo he*) means to cross the river by feeling the stones. Applying the right principles at the right time and in the right way to achieve a higher purpose represents wisdom in Chinese thinking.

Relationships play a greater role with a stronger need to "take care" of one another. Ambiguity is also tolerated as it gives room for flexible manoeuvring. In this example, the local management draws on principles of business success, greater good and relationships in a bid to manage the tension between business objectives and people concerns.

However, as Dave and the local management's approaches are different, the lack of understanding leads to frustration, mistrust and ultimately failure. We can draw a line, separate and say, "This is how the West or the East works" and compartmentalise

the different worlds. Individuals compartmentalise as well – "I behave this way in China and another way in the US". Compartmentalisation is a convenient but incomplete response.

We operate across cultures in globalised economies with collaboration between East and West. Without seeing the wholeness of our East and West perspectives, we miss the opportunity to find holistic solutions. The Institute for the Future lists social intelligence and cross-cultural competency as amongst the top 10 skills required in 2020, because people increasingly need to collaborate across cultures.[7] Similarly, Ranker, Huang and McLeod, in their book *Global Mindset Leadership*, have argued for the need to be aware of others' cultures, to be flexible, and to suspend cultural assumptions when necessary as a way of operating across different cultures. Knowing both East and West cultures helps leaders to draw from both to develop fuller perspectives on issues. In today's East-meets-West environment, how can we operate with and leverage our differences for the greater good?

THE TRUE COST OF FRAGMENTATION

What are the consequences of these situations? Fragmentation robs us of the possibility of wholeness. Being busy and feeling as if we're constantly running on a treadmill becomes a convenient excuse not to dive deeper and find wholeness in our spirit, thoughts and actions. This avoidance has consequences for our individual and collective sense of fulfilment, as well as for our physical, mental and spiritual health.

At an individual level, prolonged periods of stress lead to burnout or illness, a fact borne out in a variety of statistics gathered on the billions of dollars lost each year through diminished productivity and health-related absences. Employee surveys

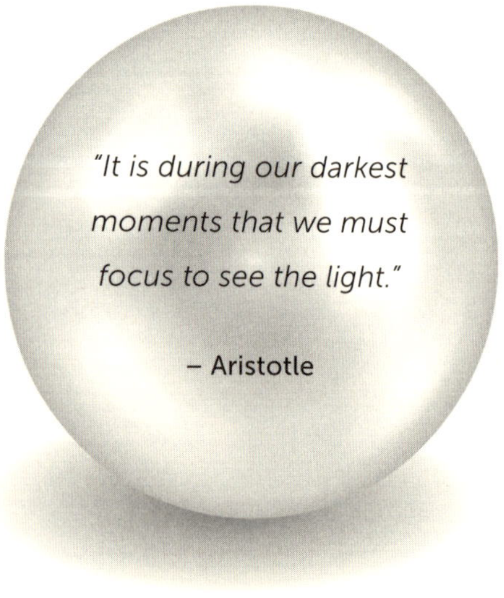

have revealed that work-related stress, depression and anxiety account for an estimated 1.8 million lost workdays a year in Britain.[8] Employees report symptoms such as headaches, high blood pressure, disturbed sleep and negative emotions. The longer-term consequences include:

- Lowered productivity
- Diminished creativity
- Life/work imbalance
- Negative health implications
- Frustrated potential
- Lingering job dissatisfaction
- Lack of needed personal time

At the organisation level, this translates into increased staff turnover and hostility as well as reduced performance and morale. Gallup reports that seven out of ten Americans in the workforce are disengaged on the job. It estimates this crisis costs the U.S. economy US$450 billion in lost productivity a year.[9] In Singapore alone, this cost is US$6 billion.[10]

At their worst, organisations are experienced as cold, soulless machines in which employees are treated as mere resources that keep the cogs moving. Work dehumanises the employees,

with frequent retrenchment exercises flushing "excessive resources" from the system.

More commonly, this kind of living prompts us to focus on the parts rather than the whole. The divide-and-conquer thinking in organisations assumes that when each department focuses on its specialised role, it will contribute along with the other departments and eventually benefit the whole. So people work in silos where they focus on their own areas without considering the effect on the whole – the larger organisation. This leads to disempowerment with too many fingers in the decision-making pie and lack of accountability on what falls in between specific areas.

Wholeness is ultimately about the health of a community, the larger organisation and even one's neighbourhood, town or city. The community is not whole if all forms of help are outsourced or left to the government to provide, suggesting that relationships are distanced at the community level. Rather, mutual help between neighbours and friends creates a more sustainable support system.

The questions that dominate the environment we work in now are:

- What provides the highest return on our investments?
- What is the fastest way to reach our financial goals?
- What is the most efficient way to reach those goals?

Rationality, efficiency and technical expertise have become the primary means of achieving these results. Presuming a linear, predictable, logical and measurable future, we've developed a mechanistic and reductionist approach. We tackle any issue by breaking it down into its parts and creating a systematic structure and efficient processes, with strategies and KPIs, priorities and work plans, and everything tracked and measured zealously.

What are the results? From a positive standpoint, this approach has enhanced our material quality of life and improved the profit margins of large corporations. Because of it, the world has seen marvellous innovations in engineering, technology and medicine. The Industrial Revolution made it possible to automate the production of large quantities of consumer goods for mass consumption. The Wright brothers' experiments in flight have evolved into today's jets and spaceships. The discovery of penicillin and other drugs has saved millions of lives. With the invention of the internet and other advancements, various systems and processes are making replication in global markets possible.

However, this progress has also contributed to a fragmentation throughout society's structure. Leaders talk about disenchantment, disempowerment and disengagement. One CEO remarked that every year after he sets stretch targets, he and the employees work frantically to meet those goals. Then, once they achieve their projected numbers, they start all over again with more ambitious targets. In this way, they're like robots within the larger machine of capitalism.

Similarly, an IBM study involving 1,700 global CEOs suggests that as the world becomes increasingly connected, relationships rather than technical processes (such as process optimisation) will increasingly be a source of competitive advantage. In today's disruptive world, Western thought's logical, linear approach seems limited. It's time to disrupt this legacy model and create space for change.

CALL FOR WHOLENESS NOW

Job security is now probably at its lowest point as the development of new technologies disrupts traditional business models. Not only is automation replacing routine work, artificial intelligence is taking over analytical work. Globalisation opens doors to the movement of capital and machinery anywhere in the world. Companies search constantly for lowest cost and highest returns. Technology and automation change the way value is created. When researchers at LinkedIn examined the data of over 259 million member profiles, they found that many popular job titles in 2014 didn't even exist in 2008[11]. So employees have less control over their work as they face nagging uncertainty about how these rapid changes could affect their jobs. To stay relevant in the global economy, professionals must constantly learn, then *un*learn and *re*learn new skills. How can we find energy to do this when we are constantly on the treadmill?

Many people work, as I did, like hamsters on a wheel, dealing with an unending list of tasks. What does this result in? Over time, our internal resources are depleted, and it becomes near impossible to attend to our purpose, be engaged in our work or muster energy to be creative and learn. This means lost opportunities to serve customers better, solve problems creatively,

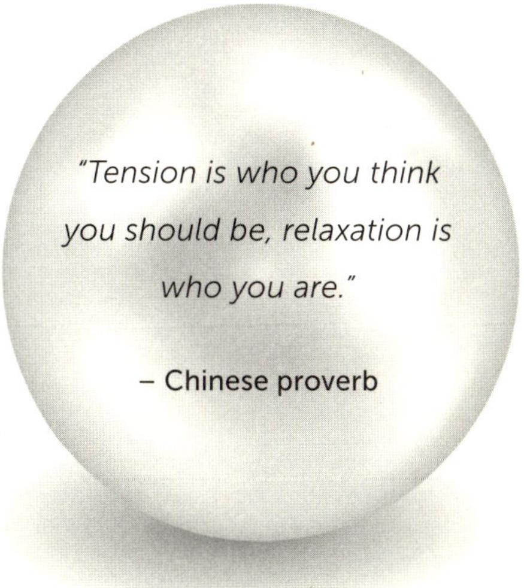

find meaning in work, and grow as human beings. The frenetic "doing" fragments our attention and energy, robbing us of both the capacity to feel whole and the desire to care for a larger community. Most significant is the loss of our spirit at work – our mindset becomes "I'm just hanging in here to make a living". In this constant *doing*, we forget about our *being*.

OVER TO YOU

Barriers to Wholeness

This is the first applied exercise. The purpose of these "Over to You" segments is for you to pause and reflect on how these ideas apply in your context and in turn generate insights that will shift you towards more wholeness in your life. You will find these segments at the end of each chapter. For now, let's start with identifying the barriers to your achieving wholeness.

1. What saps your energy?

2. What splits your attention?

3. What pulls you in different directions?

4. Review the list of barriers to your experience of wholeness every day. Tick off those that apply to you, and you may also elaborate in the spaces provided:

- ☐ Workload:
- ☐ Change(s):
- ☐ Job security:
- ☐ Technology:
- ☐ Office politics:
- ☐ Relationships:
- ☐ Lack of exercise:
- ☐ Lack of (mental) space:
- ☐ Health:
- ☐ Family:

- ☐ Uncertainty about the future:

- ☐ Not doing what you really want:

- ☐ Constantly on the hamster wheel:

- ☐ Conflicting demands:

- ☐ Lack of meaning in work:

- ☐ Any others:

As you think about these barriers to wholeness, notice for a moment how you are feeling, the thoughts on your mind and any physical sensations in your body:

Being able to identify these barriers to wholeness is a sign of being alive! You may feel a need for quick solutions. However, hold off any knee-jerk reactions. Awareness is the first step. Dive deeper to find meaningful perspectives to reframe these challenges to shift towards more wholeness.

CHAPTER 2
THE JOYS OF WHOLENESS

"Work is where the self meets the world."
– David Whyte

To find out more about wholeness, I spoke to several leaders and professionals who have successful and fulfilling lives in the global arena, an understanding of Eastern and Western perspectives and insightful views on wholeness. I share the stories of Andrew, Claire, Yin Cheng and David because they have inspired my understanding of wholeness.

Andrew Matthews – Dynamic Rebalancing

"Why do I want to be a different person at work from who I am with my family?" asks Andrew Matthews. Based in Australia,

Andrew is a chief actuary and has a master's degree in organisation development. When I ask him what wholeness means to him, he replies, "Being true to myself in all situations."

"This attitude, however, is frequently tested by the pressures and stresses at work," says Andrew. He relates an experience when his team faced a challenge from the senior executives, stakeholders and board members, who wanted critical answers on the company's capital management strategy and target capital levels. "I could pretend we had the answer – that is, a technical problem with a technical solution. But we realised this approach would focus too much on the fixed estimate and not enough on the risks, issues and tradeoffs. The alternative was to speak truth to power and risk the anxiety that 'I don't have the answer'." Andrew and team faced an adaptive problem.

In that moment, in the board room, Andrew recalled his experience surfing in the ocean. Surfing requires balancing the board and embracing the force of the waves. Despite the anxiety he felt at being regarded as a technical expert without *the* answer, he embraced the tension and admitted to the executives, board members and key stakeholders, "We don't have an answer, but we have a process that will help us get there." He referred to the Chinese saying to cross the river by feeling the stones, "摸石头过河" (*mo shi tou guo he*), and developing the answers along the way.

Andrew explains this thinking. "When I am whole, I am more able to attend to others' needs, but I also realise that I cannot be whole if others are not." Because the capital management strategy carried implications and tradeoffs for multiple stakeholders, Andrew and his team held one-on-one discussions to understand their concerns and develop a strategy that everyone could support. That way, they avoided assuming the issue was purely technical. They began working through a messy problem by using an agreed-upon process to address multiple concerns.

To Andrew, wholeness means "being true to himself *with others involved*". It's not an individualistic self-assertion; rather, it involves a sense of caring for others as part of a whole. He adds: "Wholeness is also active, not static." Thus people can't "arrive" at wholeness and remain there. Using surfing as an analogy, he strives to experience wholeness as a dynamic rebalancing amid the waves of anxiety and change.

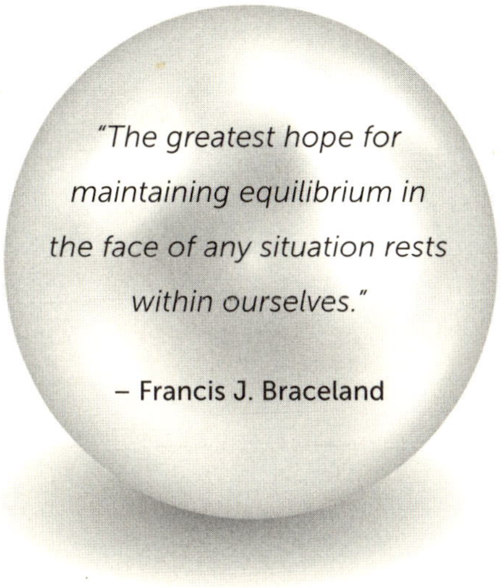

Claire Chiang – Strong "I" and "We"

"Committed, courageous, compassionate Claire," I thought after speaking to Claire Chiang. She acts with a conviction stemming from her values and principles, and integrates strategies from both East and West in her thinking.

Claire has made impressive achievements in her business, social, political and personal life. She co-founded the exclusive Banyan Tree Hotels & Resorts, which employs 12,000 people of 16 nationalities from five continents. She also developed more than 60 Banyan Tree retail outlets worldwide. Most impressively, Claire was one of the first two women elected to the board of the Singapore Chinese Chamber of Commerce and Industry, which had been dominated by male leaders for nearly a century.

Claire also serves numerous causes she cares about, including the environment, education, and women's and children's

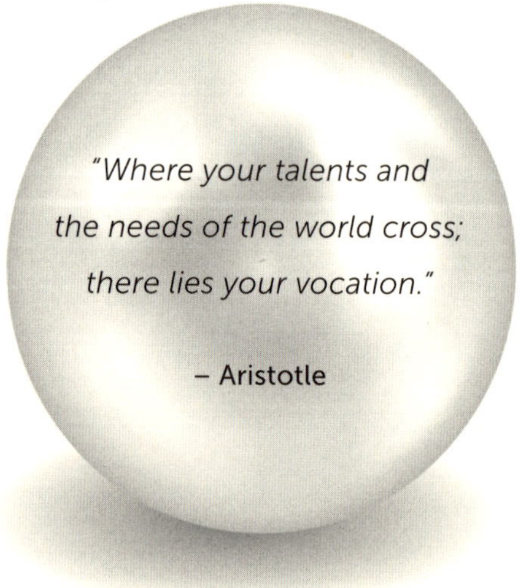

issues. In 2014, she received the Public Service Star (BBM) for her contribution to implementing work-life integration as part of Singapore's commitment to create a fair, responsible and progressive work environment. In addition, she served two terms as a nominated member of Singapore's parliament, during which she raised many social-sector policy issues.

Claire's family is very important to her. Married and the mother of three, she put off completing her PhD studies to care for her ailing mother-in-law, changing the course of her career.

With so many passions and responsibilities, how does Claire manage to have wholeness in all spheres of her life? She responds quickly with clarity: "We need a strong 'I' to influence the 'we'. As my mother used to say, '天生我才必有用' (*tian sheng wo cai bi you yong*) – since we are born into this world, we must develop our talents and be useful."

Breaking out into occasional Mandarin idioms, evidence of her Chinese upbringing, Claire says, "随欲勇取 (*sui yu yong qu*) – this means in life, we should take action and not just let things pass." Claire firmly believes in self-agency. "I act and know that I must also have courage to assume responsibility. It's heavy for me. Still, I have chosen to do all this work because I love and care about my family, work, people, friends and country. Contributing to the community is integral to all aspects of my life."

A self-declared friend of all religions, Claire searches for the common goodness in people. She explains, "While we dig

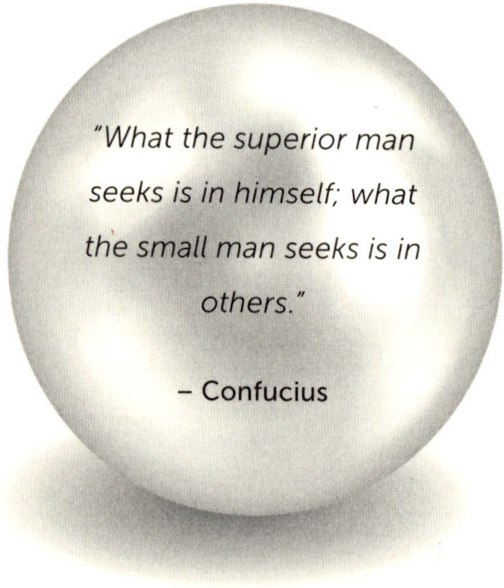

different wells and have different religions, we touch the same bottom line – the wellspring of humanity, 真善美 (*zhen shan mei*, 'truth, compassion, and beauty'). Honesty, loyalty, love, service to community and filial piety are values that we all embrace."

This unyielding core comes through in the consistency of Claire's actions. "言行一致 (*yan xing yi zhi*) means 'what you say is what you do,'" she adds with a swift gesturing of her hands. I ask her about the concept of an anchor that roots us. She replies: "Through the clarity of our anchor, we align the way we live, work and conduct business, so our values are aligned across different contexts: self, family, community and the world."

Claire draws from both Eastern and Western cultures to have wholeness in her thinking. "Singapore has a unique strength in our Western education and Asian culture. This East-West integration permits us to draw from both wells: the West's rationalism and Asia's wisdom." For example, while Claire is uncompromising in her principles and values, she demonstrates great flexibility in her actions. "I like the chaotic, blurred, hesitant, non-committal nature of the Chinese ways because that gives me a wider margin in which to play, learn and find common ground. Of course, Western ways have strengths, too."

"I do what the situation requires of me, so I can be effective," she emphasises with an undertone of strength. "If I'm in a situation where the people around me cannot accept a strong, opinionated and instructive personality, that creates distance between us, and I am not effective. Either I change, or they change. Since I can't change others, I will change myself."

Claire's adaptability results in an impressive tolerance for partnerships and the dynamics of change. "When the core, cognition and context are all aligned, we grow in the journey and develop from this positive energy," she says. This is how she works across different spheres – personal, business, political and social – to create positive impact.

Lau Yin Cheng – Flexibility in Formlessness

"Wholeness incorporates the connections and patterns among individuals, teams and an organisation in the form of relationships, information flow and context. Seeing these connections helps us make effective change," Lau Yin Cheng, a human resources director and organisation development practitioner, explains over coffee in a café overlooking the shimmering bay on a late evening.

Seeing himself as an instrument of change, he seeks to "be present in the moment and be a present to the system". He shares an example: "Department restructurings are often fraught with complex dynamics amongst the people involved. There's a need to delineate needs, strengths and personalities as well as the ever-evolving demands of the organisation. A typical approach would be to examine best practices and logical frameworks, and then put employees into the right areas."

Yin Cheng tosses his head back and confesses he used to be a "framework" kind of guy – analytical and logical. "Frameworks provide a sense of predictability and mastery. They are useful initially in the learning process. However, we should not let frameworks cage our thinking. In fact, the greatest form is actually formlessness." This formlessness allows the dynamics of the people and the situation to integrate so the needs of people are identified and an adaptive evolution can take place.

"For example, the dynamics of people and the system affect the success of any initiative in powerful ways," he says. So he engages his team members one-on-one to understand their concerns and aspirations. In the process, he gains insights on every member's wants and fears. With sufficient data points, he diagnoses the team dynamics and integrates the data to pinpoint the path of least resistance. To help them see the big picture, he facilitates conversations among team members about any upcoming changes. Further one-on-one conversations take place to close the loop as the new structure takes form. This approach has consistently helped him solve thorny issues in a harmonious way with the least amount of angst and effort.

> *"Empty your mind, be formless. Shapeless, like water. Now, water can flow or it can crash. Be water, my friend."*
>
> **– Bruce Lee**

To Yin Cheng, being good at this "formless" approach to change requires managers to have three key abilities: (1) a high emotional and intellectual aptitude that helps them understand the needs and fears of their people; (2) a non-judgmental perspective that allows them to calmly assess situations; and (3) a deep understanding of their own fears, needs and emotions so they can be of service.

Despite the whirling change around him, Yin Cheng exudes a calm aura with clarity in his thinking. "If we want to be instruments of change, we must understand that our perceptions of the situation are critical to influencing our thoughts, feelings and subsequent actions," he explains. "Our emotions decide the data we receive. Empathising with others' emotions helps us understand both the dynamics that influence actions and how the system interacts with each person."

For example, when we are angry, we easily blame others and assume the worst. Similarly, when we are fearful, we imagine threats and suspect others' intentions. But when we are calm and open, we see situations as they are and can empathise with others' situations.

As he integrates the different data points, Yin Cheng's confidence and courage grow. He realises what he needs to do next, remaining mindful of new data points as people change and new possibilities emerge. The lynchpin within this, he said, is understanding human needs and hot-button issues. "It is easy to be hooked by our ego needs to be recognised, appreciated and liked. When our need for recognition gets in the way, we think we must present ourselves positively rather than neutrally. As instruments of change, everything comes through us. Our egos colour our perceptions, emotions and actions."

He acknowledges that it takes continual self-discipline to be present in the moment. To be effective in assessing patterns, he says, means cleaning our own lenses by being aware of personal needs, fears and emotions. Consciously putting ourselves in a calm state allows us to see situations as they are and then identify what needs to be done. To stay calm and centred himself, Yin Cheng practices meditation. To him, meditation opens a window to our wisdom.

Dr. David Y.H. Chang – Taking Actions Based on Context

David Chang, originally from Taiwan, earned his master's degree and PhD in the United States. He worked in the US for many years before being tapped for the role of vice-president of technical operations at Roche Pharmaceuticals' Shanghai office. David's role is to transform the company into a leading state-of-the-art pharmaceutical manufacturing site.

David has absorbed both a Chinese sensibility from his upbringing in Taiwan and knowledge of Western management practices as a professional in the U.S. He brings both perspectives to his management style at Roche Shanghai. In fact, his blend of East and West caused one of his Chinese staffers to say, "I don't know where to place you!"

Roche Pharmaceuticals' technical operation has traditionally been led by European leaders, who tend to focus on discipline and execute in a command-and-control approach. Chinese culture, in which people tend to follow leaders' orders without challenge, reinforces this corporate culture of high-performance expectations and low tolerance for questions.

How do leaders typically tackle the need to transform a company? Many pass judgment on the current practices and introduce immediate changes. Here's a typical plan:

1. Designate new members in top management
2. Do a gap analysis
3. Define a new strategy and culture
4. Develop a plan for change management
5. Prioritise and drive projects
6. Distribute rewards based on performance

The cycle continues. Such approaches deliver results in the short-term; however, they require a lot of effort to drive them.

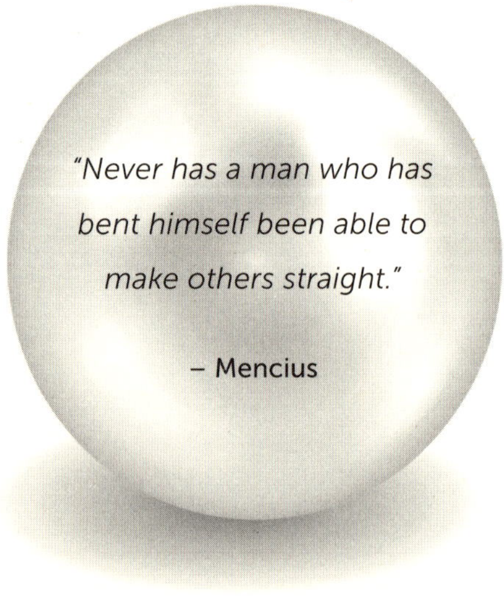

But what happens after the driver leaves? Typically the results achieved cannot be sustained without the driver.

David's approach is different. When he came to Roche Shanghai, he observed the way things worked within the organisation and how its people thought. Because he's Chinese, it was easier for David to gain understanding without passing judgment. "People here have been moulded to respect their leaders and follow instructions for a long time. It's common to judge this as blind compliance. In an attempt to change that, it's not unusual for foreign managers to use the wrong words, forcing people to speak up or calling them out on the spot," he explains. "In pushing change, a lot of effort can be expended without much response because employees are not ready; they don't know what to do or how to do it. As a result, people feel scared and confused. They begin to gossip about or criticise the leader behind his back."

To truly transform, David says, "We need to look holistically and get different angles on things. For example, to build the right behaviours in Chinese people, we need to identify many aspects of behaviour, not just one. However, we can probably only focus on one at a time, and it takes years to cultivate all these traits in the desired way."

Rather than force change, he creates opportunities for people to diagnose themselves. They experience new ways and decide the future they want for themselves, which allows them to go from seeing the change to wanting the change. "People need to analyse the root causes to build awareness and develop an internal drive for change," David explains. "When they see that's what I want as well, we start to experience engagement. Then people are happier at work and willing to do more. They will feel they have a meaningful future."

This is similar to the idea that although we cannot actually see trees grow day by day, we know they are growing, and we can see the effect over time. Within an organisation, David creates an environment for growth by igniting internal drive for change. That requires patience.

Contrast this to the strong, charismatic leader who paints a vision of the future that charges people to follow. In the way that David leads, the leader is a facilitator rather than leading the charge for change. Nevertheless, his flexibility brings awareness of the context of the situation and people involved, helping him to identify what is needed. He adds, "Sometimes, people don't know what they don't know," and this is when he needs to take a more directive approach.

David believes in leading by example and through role-modelling. For example, one of the fundamental behaviours he encourages is to ask "Why" instead of adhering to instructions without question. In his meetings, he tells his people what kinds of "why" questions to ask and the reasons they should ask them. Often, he shifts to be a change agent or champion as he acknowledges the importance of making decisions and sharing responsibility.

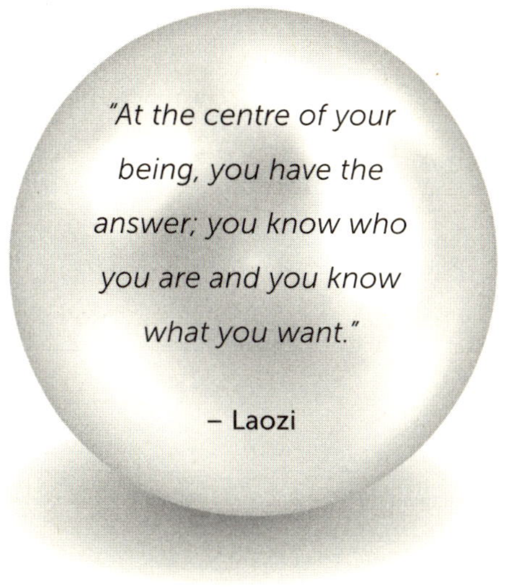

Within this interplay is the notion of blending. "Sometimes we manage by caring about them, sometimes by disciplining them. Sometimes we guide our people, and sometimes we tell them what to do. Although we have a long-term view, we use short-term tactics to create change across these polarities," he explains. Clearly, by shifting his roles based on the context and people involved, David doesn't subscribe to any fixed leadership behaviours.

David's actions are, however, guided by a larger purpose. He aims not to simply deliver business results but to develop his people, acting as the bridge to bring them and the organisation into a new age. "Earlier in my career, I focused on making ends meet, learning, trying new things and fulfilling my intellectual curiosity. Now, after 27 years, I think about giving. By going beyond just making ends meet, I hope to contribute to others."

> *"Kindness is more important than wisdom. The recognition of this is the beginning of wisdom."*
>
> – Theodore Rubin

A year after David started this journey, his company reported significant improvement – as much as a 45-percent increase in employee engagement. Employees are more optimistic and clear about their futures, and demonstrate the desired behaviours within a culture that their leader intended to develop.

David's anchor includes his purpose, values, identity and responsibilities. He embraces polarities in his thinking and acts based on the context. Knowing that transformation takes time, he is patient with the change process, and is comfortable with the creative tension in the existing situation.

THE COMMON THREADS OF WHOLENESS

The stories above describe four people who have put wholeness to use in all aspects of their lives. All of them have a clear sense of who they are and their connection to the larger community around them. There is both strong "I" and "We". Clarity about her values and responsibilities directed Claire with consistent actions across the different spheres of business, family and community. Andrew was committed to being his authentic self at work and at home and strove to be whole together with his larger community – his colleagues and family.

In addition, they are comfortable navigating polarities and also letting go of prescribed frameworks. Guided by his purpose of giving back, David approaches his staff with non-judgment and takes appropriate actions based on the context. Yin Cheng, regarding himself as a positive agent of change, seeks to be whole in the moment, to see himself and others in a situation clearly, so that he is not restricted by any particular form of solution or prescribed structure. This gives him flexibility to adapt.

CONNECTION WITH THE SELF AND THE LARGER WORLD

In the stories of Andrew, Claire, Yin Cheng and David, a common thread we find is seeing wholeness as a connection with oneself and with the larger world:

Connection with the Self:	Connection with Others and the Larger World:
• *"Being true to myself."*	• *"I cannot be whole if others are not."*
• *"Strong 'I' – through the clarity of who we are, we align the ways we live, work and conduct business as well as who we do business with."*	• *"Choosing to do all this work because I love and care about my family, work, people, friends and country."*
• *"Beyond making ends meet, I hope to contribute to others."*	• *"Create an environment for growth by igniting internal drive for change."*
• *"Stay calm and centred – be present in the moment."*	• *"Understand that the dynamics of the people and the system affect the success of any initiative in powerful ways."*

Participants in my wholeness workshops share similar responses:

Connection with the Self:

- *"There was an alignment of mind, body, and spirit."*
- *"When I am dancing, I feel connected with myself again."*
- *"I was being myself and felt authentic in my own skin."*

Connection with Others and the Larger World:

- *"I felt we were together as a team. We were supporting one another, and it was beautiful."*
- *"I realised how connected I am with everyone else."*
- *"I felt a sense of co-existence with nature and of blending into everything else."*

These ideas show a consistent pattern about connecting more deeply with oneself and the larger world.

OVER TO YOU

Moments of Wholeness

Think about a time when you felt whole, deeply fulfilled and at peace. It could be at work, in nature or in your everyday life. It may have lasted for only a moment or much longer. It could be something simple or more major. Whatever the situation, you experienced a sense of balance and completeness. Describe the situation. When did it take place? What was happening? What were you doing? How did you feel? What was on your mind then? Feel free to write or draw in the space below.

As you reflect on your moment of wholeness, how do you feel? What thoughts come to mind? What sensations do you feel in your body?

Compare this to the time when you were reflecting on the barriers to wholeness in Chapter 1. What is the difference?

CHAPTER 3
HOW WHOLENESS WORKS

"When we seek for connection, we restore the world to wholeness. Our seemingly separate lives become meaningful as we discover how truly necessary we are to each other."
– Margaret Wheatley

In searching for representative images of wholeness, I discovered several:

- **A baby sleeping blissfully.** She is whole because she is at peace, clear and complete with her needs, unaware of what others think of her and unencumbered with responsibilities.

- **A circle.** With no start or end, this shape represents a continuity that has no bias for any portion. This definition comes from the Chinese perspective, 圆满 (*yuan man*), which translates as "complete circle". Its completeness connotes wholeness.

- **An obituary photograph.** As morbid as it might seem, in many ways death brings completeness. Photos of people who have died remind us that they have come full circle in life and now rest in peace.

- **A seed.** A seed holds enormous potential within a tiny container. It must patiently await the passage of time for its life to unfold, bringing its full blossom to the larger world as a contribution.

- **A Mobius strip.** Similar to the infinity sign, one side of the strip integrates into the other side endlessly.

As seeds or babies, we are whole. But as time passes, we become anxious about what our parents, friends or bosses think of us. We care about how we look or perform; what we will accomplish in life; how we will make money; what kind of house or car we will own; how our children's futures will unfold, and so on. Then finally, at the end of our lives, we are whole again because whatever is simply *is*.

We come into the world whole and leave it whole, but a huge part of the journey can easily be fraught with anxieties. The message of this book is about being whole on this journey, so that we can be our best and do our best sustainably.

WHOLENESS AS THIRDNESS

We may think of wholeness as the sum of its parts. However, true wholeness occurs when the parts come together to create something more expansive and life-giving than the individual parts – a powerful synergy.

Consider these:

- Breathe in + Breathe out = Life energy
- Push + Pull = Movement
- I + You = We
- Give + Take = Collaboration

- Harmony + Conflict = Genuine relationship
- Truth + Care = Trust
- Attach + Detach = Move forward
- Balance + Imbalance = Dynamic equilibrium
- Capitalism + Community = Socially responsible and caring business
- Realism + Idealism = Pragmatism
- Business + Relationship = Long-term partnership
- Firm principles + Rounded application = Harmony with principles
- Decision based on logic + Care in relationship = Reasonable actions
- Eastern values + Western know-how = Sustainable development
- East + West = Global

In all of these examples, the individual components come together to create something larger. The whole is greater than the sum of its parts. The complementary but opposing polarities described in the *yin-yang* philosophy are common knowledge.

> *"Every great and deep difficulty bears in itself its own solution. It forces us to change our thinking in order to find it."*
>
> **– Niels Bohr**

We know there is no light without darkness. But consider a more subtle notion: light and darkness come together to create a cycle of day and night, a rhythm of life. This is a *thirdness*, a wholeness created from the integration of light and dark.

Thirdness is not a simple addition of two polarities. I learnt from being a swim mum that swimming actually consists of exertion and relaxation. Pete, my eldest son, learns to relax his hand when it is out of the water and glide in effortlessly, whilst pushing effortfully under water to propel himself forward. He would not be able to sustain long distances if he exerted all the time! Similarly, when riding a bicycle, one leg pushes and the other pulls, and together they create movement and balance. There is no movement if both legs push against the pedals at the same time.

A tea custom of a minority Chinese tribe helped me understand this further. The Baizu tribe drinks tea in three courses – bitter, sweet, and aftertaste. The first tea is bitter, because the tribe believes that we need to put in effort, to experience the trials and tribulations in life, before we can experience the sweetness that results from the fruits of our efforts. That is represented by the second tea, which is also sweet. The third tea is most interesting. It tastes bitter, sweet, sour and spicy – all at the same time. As I drank it, it was rich and full-bodied, with a lingering aftertaste. This tea is aptly called "aftertaste" because the meaning is to savour one's bitter and sweet experiences and realise the wisdom and learning acquired in the process. The thirdness from one's efforts (bitter) and subsequent rewards (sweet) is the learning and maturity acquired on one's journey. So thirdness is the result of a fusion of parts that is more expansive and life-giving than any of the parts on their own. This is also wholeness. We can also think of two metals being mixed together. An alloy, stronger than either component, is created.

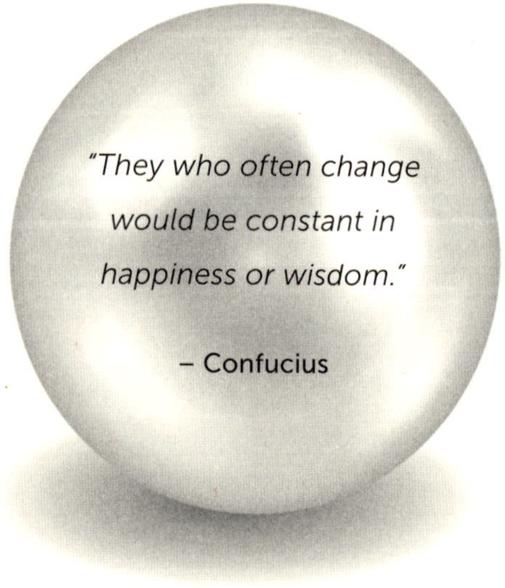

Many of us tend to view life from an "either-or" perspective. Democracy or authoritarianism. Business or community. Career or family. Every social, business, or personality construct has a counter-force to complete it, resulting in thirdness. Seeing the necessity of both perspectives helps us understand where each of us comes from. Integrating the other perspective helps us to be whole in our thinking and to put forth our best ideas for that context. For individuals, as professionals, leaders, parents, or spouses, becoming whole in our thinking helps us make wise decisions for ourselves, our teams, families and community. For organisations, wholeness in our thinking helps us manage polarities and search for creative solutions to create sustainable success.

WHOLENESS WEST AND EAST

Traditionally, Western societies focus more on individual wholeness, while Eastern societies emphasise the collective. Richard E. Nisbett, author of *Geography of Thought*[12], provides insight on the "I" and "we" dimensions. In one of his research projects, he asked American and Japanese students to describe animated videos of underwater scenes. Americans were more likely to start by mentioning the subject, which included the prominent objects such as brightly coloured fish and aquatic plants, while the vast majority of Japanese students talked about the context, such as how the scene looked. They also mentioned more relationships between the objects and the environment.

> *"You can tell whether a person is clever by his answers. You can tell whether a person is wise by his questions."*
>
> **– Mahfouz Naguib**

Similarly, using eye-tracking equipment and a picture of a tiger in a jungle, Nisbett found that Americans tended to look at the tiger (the subject) more quickly and focus on it for a longer time. The Chinese participants, on the other hand, flicked their gaze more often between the animal and the background.[13]

Nisbett noted that Westerners tend to see objects and the space between them as having no influence on each other. Put another way, separation and categorisation of objects is central to Western thinking. The properties of objects or the personalities of individuals determine the outcome. Thus, wholeness from the Western context focuses on individuals as intact entities.

This concept of wholeness is about people being happy, true to themselves and free to lead the lives they want. An Amazon search on books related to wholeness yields dozens of results on personal discovery, becoming more of oneself, recovery from trauma, and spirituality. A psychology self-help book by Parker Palmer, *A Hidden Wholeness: The Journey Toward An Undivided Life*[14], explores the idea of the authentic self. Similarly, "Let It Go", the theme song from the movie *Frozen*, reflects this notion of individual wholeness – letting go of what others expect me to be, being free, and being my "true self".

On the other hand, Nisbett's observations of Easterners revealed a tendency to focus on the environment, context and relationships. He rationalised that Easterners recognise the space between objects as key and understand that each individual and object possesses *qi* (气), or life force. The *qi* of objects interact with one another to create an outcome. For example, infertility treatments in the West are scientific and highly targeted. With in vitro fertilisation, egg and sperm are extracted for external fertilisation, before transferring back to the uterus for further development. On the other hand, traditional Chinese medicine (TCM), with its basis in *qi*, *yin-yang* and the Five Elements, does not treat the ailment directly. Instead, TCM practitioners use acupuncture and herbs to harmonise the *qi* movements in the five organs (liver, heart, spleen, lungs and kidney), thus creating the conditions for natural conception to take place. So Easterners recognise that the surroundings and relationships, on top of the entities themselves, are important in influencing outcomes.

For Asians, rather than individuals being central, the relationships among individuals become key. Thus, wholeness arises from the relationships between the people and their natural surroundings and social systems. Wholeness comes from harmony in these relationships. The Chinese term for wholeness is 完整 (*wan zheng*, which means completeness).

Coming from Singapore, the nexus between East and West, we are neither East nor West, but both. I was raised with Chinese values but immersed in Western know-how. The growth of Singapore from third world to first in 50 years was shaped not only by our founding prime minister, Mr Lee Kuan Yew, but also by navigating between East and West to find our third way. This book seeks to articulate this thirdness, so that we are more aware of what we are creating and intentionally navigating through both polarities to have more wholeness.

WESTERN MIND, ASIAN HEART

Here's an example of East/West wholeness at the organisational level. Formed in 2000, CapitaLand has become one of Asia's largest real estate companies, with about 12,000 staff and over 500 properties in more than 20 countries. Being a Singapore-founded multinational corporation, CapitaLand integrates Western logic with an Asian heart.

CapitaLand's management processes, derived from Western practices, are structured and data-driven. In the pursuit of growth, CapitaLand uses the Balanced Scorecard approach, where strategy and goals are translated to performance outcomes comprising both quantitative and qualitative targets. These goals are broken down based on the responsibilities of the various departments and cascaded down throughout the organisation, thereby creating alignment across the board. This "breaking the whole into parts" is a classic Western management approach. In addition, there are clear policies guiding employees on how to do their work. Drawing on Western-originated governance practices, integrity is a cornerstone of the company's values. CapitaLand takes a firm stand against corruption, with all staff being required to sign an anti-corruption pledge every year.[15]

On the other hand, CapitaLand's Asian heart is represented by the values of hard work, loyalty and care for people. Instead of retrenchments, Capitaland's management team took a double-digit pay cut in 2009 during the Global Financial Crisis to preserve jobs. This reinforced the loyalty of the staff, with 43% of CapitaLand staff having been in the company for at least five years. In response to disruptive changes, Lim Ming Yan, the

President and Group CEO, takes a "traditional Chinese medicine" approach to steer the organisation forward – active education on the future of real estate, clear vision on what CapitaLand needs to do differently, and articulation of the skills required. In this way, Capitaland gives the relevant "tonic" to create the environment for staff to develop the needed capabilities. This contrasts with the swift hire-and-fire approach typical in more Western-oriented restructuring exercises.

By drawing on the best of Eastern and Western practices, CapitaLand has won awards for architectural design, sustainable green standards in buildings, and innovative services, living up to its credo of building people and communities.

"I" AND "WE" WHOLENESS

Claire Chiang explained that "I" and "We" coexist and strengthen each other. Bringing "I" and "We" together is wholeness, both for the individual and collective. Consider the leaf of a tree. The leaf and stem attach to the branch, the branch is joined to the trunk, and the trunk leads to the roots. An individual is like a leaf, connected to the rest of the tree – the family, team or organisation, and the community. Beyond the leaf, the tree is the larger whole.

The leaf can only be healthy if the tree is healthy. Similarly, the individual is more likely to be whole if his family, team and community are healthy. In the same vein, as individuals we contribute to the well-being of our communities – that is, we make one another whole.

Extending the analogy of a tree, wholeness is rooted in Mother Earth. In fact, all plants, living things and matter are part of Mother Earth. As a result, this form of wholeness expands beyond teams, organisations, and communities to include all humanity, nature, and the planet itself.

When we recognise the importance of wholeness beyond ourselves, we learn to act in ways that nurture and sustain the larger whole. Picture a congested roadway. Some drivers are oblivious to everyone else around them. Others pay close attention and show courtesy, allowing other drivers to manoeuvre easily. For example, in a traffic jam, a mindful driver might inch his car as far forward as possible to allow the vehicle behind to make a turn. Inching the car forward doesn't create a loss for that driver, but it's a huge gain for someone else. This shows a consciousness of others beyond oneself.

At work, wholeness involves an individual's commitment to serve the organisation because the interests of both are intertwined. It is a willingness to be a citizen and a desire to leave a place better than it was when we found it.

A number of enlightened entrepreneurs and leaders are role models in balancing individual and collective wholeness. They've shown that their company's brand image has more credibility when they carry out the meaning of their company's marketing through their treatment of employees and community. When consumers see a corporate philosophy that brings together workforce and community, they respond with loyalty. Consider the case of Costco, as reported in *Bloomberg Businessweek*:

> Costco Wholesale, the second-largest retailer in the U.S. behind Walmart, is an anomaly in an age marked by turmoil and downsizing. Known for its $55-a-year membership fee and its massive, austere warehouses stocked floor to ceiling with indulgent portions of everything from tilapia to toilet paper, Costco has thrived over the last five years. While competitors lost customers to the Internet and weathered a wave of investor pessimism, Costco's sales have grown 39 percent and its stock price has doubled since 2009. The hot streak continued through last year's retirement of widely admired co-founder and Chief Executive Officer Jim Sinegal. The share price is up 30 percent under the leadership of its new, plain-spoken CEO, Craig Jelinek.
>
> Despite the sagging economy and challenges to the industry, Costco pays its hourly workers an average of $20.89 an hour,

> not including overtime (vs. the minimum wage of $7.25 an hour). By comparison, Walmart said its average wage for full-time employees in the U.S. is $12.67 an hour, according to a letter it sent in April to activist Ralph Nader. Eighty-eight percent of Costco employees have company-sponsored health insurance; Walmart says that "more than half" of its employees do. Costco workers with coverage pay premiums that amount to less than 10 percent of the overall cost of their plans. It treats its employees well in the belief that a happier work environment will result in a more profitable company. "I just think people need to make a living wage with health benefits," says Jelinek. "It also puts more money back into the economy and creates a healthier country. It's really that simple."

We make each other whole. Wholeness in the collective engenders a sense of abundance, a belief that there is enough for

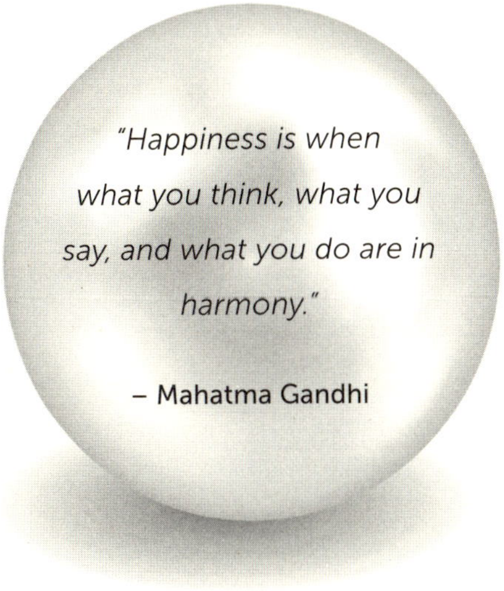

everyone, confidence that we can get through together, and comfort that the world is a good place. In the U.S., the non-religious holiday Thanksgiving has this effect on people. It is a time when people reconnect as family, and citizens of various political persuasions all agree on the importance of focusing on hunger and poverty.

WHOLENESS AS A PROCESS

Wholeness is not a destination, a place like nirvana that we arrive at and simply stay in. It is dynamic, with different levels, much like a spiral. We experience wholeness in the moment in everyday life, because now is all we have. When that happens, in that moment, we feel calm, at peace and wiser.

Andrew Matthews, whom you met in Chapter 2, says, "I try to realise more quickly that I am not whole so I rebalance quickly. A martial arts master once said to me, the difference between a white belt and black belt is the ability to recognise off-balance more quickly." The awareness that we are unbalanced leads us to rebalance ourselves. The quicker we realise this, the easier we regain wholeness in the moment.

A surf board lying on the sand is evenly balanced. But there is no energy or movement or fun. In the water, with the moving waves, we are constantly off-balance, and we need to balance and rebalance on the wobbling surf board. Similarly in *taiji*, if we place 50:50 weight on both feet, this equilibrium is also dead weight, with no movement or progress.

So to be balanced, we need to be first unbalanced. It is not a stationary state. Similarly, the lack of wholeness propels us towards wholeness. In fact, if we experience wholeness all the time, then possibly we are living too safe a life. When we are totally whole at the end of our lives, we are also dead.

In experiencing wholeness, we also have moments when we don't feel whole. These two states are mirror images and both are necessary. For example, in writing this book, there were moments of clarity when the writing simply flowed. At other times, I felt as clear as mud and was fraught with uncertainty. I reminded myself to embrace the anxiety as I sought to rebalance myself by getting a drink or exercising. In the process, I become calmer and clearer. Clarity and confusion, calm and anxiety, are all part of the creative process.

As we continuously rebalance ourselves, over time, like a seed unfolding its potential, something larger and more expansive is created. Whilst unfolding in this process, we can also be complete in the moment. Rather than wait for the once-a-year vacation to finally relax and feel whole again, seek moments of wholeness in the midst of everyday work.

In summary, wholeness is the sense of completeness and balance within ourselves and the world around us. We experience wholeness in the moment. It is a dynamic continuous rebalancing process. Being whole as individuals is both a precursor and result of being whole as a community. Finally, wholeness is the thirdness created when parts come together to create something more expansive and life-giving.

OVER TO YOU

Your Personal Vision of Wholeness

1. When you think about wholeness, what images or metaphors come to mind? Sketch them below. Describe the characteristics of this image or metaphor.

2. Look at the word cloud below, identify two to four words that represent wholeness to you. Make a sentence from each word. By doing so, you create a vision of your own wholeness. Consider all aspects of your life, not just your professional role.

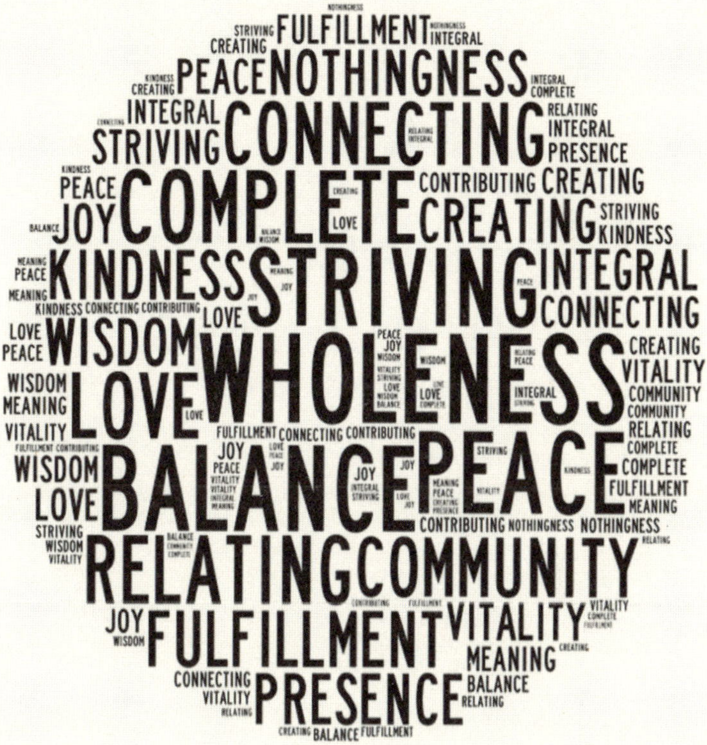

3. Record your sentences:

PART II

THE ABCs OF WHOLENESS

WHOLENESS IS A SENSE OF PEACE and completeness within oneself and with the world around. After learning from wise others, researching into Eastern and Western ways of thinking plus miles of reflection while jogging, three fundamentals of wholeness – the ABCs – became clear to me:

Anchoring: Our anchor is who we are as an individual, and who we are in relation to our world. It encapsulates our identity, values, responsibilities and purpose. Strength in our anchor provides commitment, courage and clarity.

Balancing: We balance polarities not through 50:50 compromise but via the dynamic balance of polarities 100:100 over time, creating a thirdness that is more expansive and creative.

Clearing: We empty ourselves so that we can focus on the present moment, connect to when, who and what matters. When we do this, we are whole in the moment. The sense of wholeness is dynamic and experienced in the moment.

Why these ABCs? In the face of whirling changes around us, we need to anchor ourselves and stay rooted. Taking guidance from our anchor, we balance our thinking and embrace opposing ideas, so that we are expansive in finding our solutions. With some clarity about our solutions, we empty and clear ourselves to take action.

CHAPTER 4
ANCHORING

He who knows others is learned;
He who knows himself is wise.
He who conquers others has power of muscles;
He who conquers himself is strong.
He who is contented is rich.
He who is determined has strength of will.
He who does not lose his centre endures.
He who dies yet (his power) remains has long life.
– *Dao De Jing*, Chapter 33

How does a tree grow tall and strong amidst the elements?

You're right, it's the roots. The deeper and wider the roots go, the taller and stronger the tree can be. The roots anchor the tree.

What is the parallel for individuals? What anchors you? For me, what anchors me is my role as a mother, as a professional, joy in making a difference and contributing. Anchors give us clarity about what is important, and help us stay grounded in what matters.

Early in my career, the birth of my first child, Pete, provided an extension of my anchor. I was pondering whether to return to the "safety" and "predictability" of corporate life and abandon the entrepreneurial experiment of my training and consultancy start-up. I loved to do the work, but I did not like to sell or promote. It was tough not knowing what was around the quarter, whether we would have enough work. I gave birth under subsidised care as I was worried about our cash flow. That meant I had a different doctor attending to me with every checkup. There was no continuity of relationship or someone I could build long-term trust in to deliver my child. It added to the stress of being a first-time mum.

"Personal mastery means approaching one's life as a creative work, living life from a creative as opposed to reactive viewpoint."

– Peter Senge

I never expected a little life would change my life and perspective so much. Being a mother added a new dimension to my anchor. I wanted to spend time with Pete, watch him grow, and be available to him. Clarity of this anchor made me stronger and braver. I decided failure was not an option. I had to make my experiment work. So I learnt to market, sell, write and hone my craft. This is a story about my anchor – what about others?

Aaron Maniam, a director in the Singapore civil service, talks about how people can bring their whole selves to a public service career.[16] "Given my highly mixed family background, I have learnt to transcend easy labels and categories and realise that each of us is more than the sum of our component identities." Beyond ethnic identities, Aaron identifies the different dimensions of himself coming together in service of the larger whole. Being a poet, volunteer university lecturer, activist and leader in not one but several community organisations all contribute to his current role. Perspectives gained from one dimension add depth to the others.

But how does he juggle all this? Does he compartmentalise his different roles? How does he stay whole? "By seeing the big picture from the parts together. It took me a while to figure out, but now I am clearer that my greater self is about growing and contributing to others' growth. There are days where I even wonder if I would be a better teacher than policy-maker, but on most days I realise that one of the most important things we can do (as public servants) is to teach each other and ensure knowledge, skills and experience are shared and reinforced. So my different roles are aligned to this purpose."

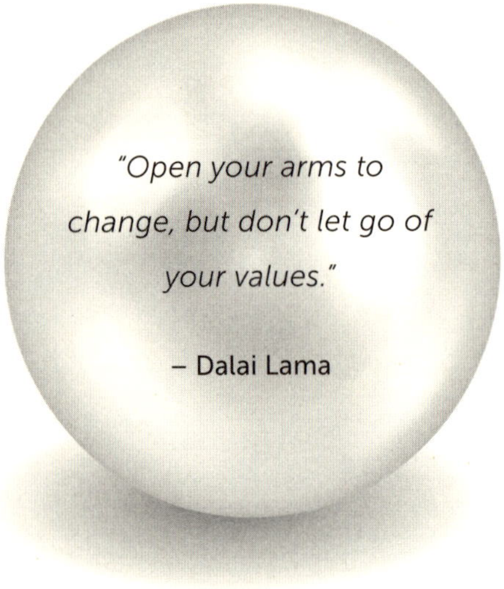

Aaron maintains coherence between these roles and the fuller picture of his wholeness. Rather than compartmentalise behaviours in different situations, this personal clarity helps him stay congruent and be whole.

THE ASPECTS OF OUR ANCHOR

One tiny seed contains the possibility of a majestic tree. Similarly, our anchor captures the essence of who we are. There are two dimensions to our anchor:

1. Who am I, as an individual? This relates to our identity and values. What matters to me? What do I want? This is also about being comfortable with who am I as an individual.

2. Who am I, in relation to my community – my family, organisation, neighbourhood, country and larger world? This refers to our relation to the people around us, our responsibilities and purpose.

To explore your anchor, consider the following questions:

1. **Values.** What do you value in your life and work? What kind of person do you want to be? What is important to you? Values guide your behaviours and help you make decisions. Are you clear about your values, or do you flow according to societal norms? For me, I make decisions on work assignments based on whether I will learn something new more than on how much pay I will receive. Learning, wisdom, generosity, compassion and relationships matter more to me. What about you?

2. **Identity.** At one level, identity is about the roles we have – job title and family role(s). These are important, but we also need to go one step further and ask, "Who am I without all my roles, job title, and expertise?" How you see yourself determines how you think and what you do. A key element of my identity is an explorer. I am curious about ideas, people and the world out there. This drives me to venture out in search of new experiences, ideas, cultures and people. What about you? What is a key word that describes your core identity?

3. **Purpose.** If you had only six months to live, what would you say is most important to you? For most people, family

is paramount. Beyond that, this question prompts you to consider what you are on Earth to do, what is meaningful to you. Some people might consider this a spiritual question, but it's as practical as it is spiritual. Knowing or deciding what you are here to do puts you on task. For example, part of what I am here to do is to be a good mother and to be of service to others. What is your purpose?

4. **Responsibility.** What are your core responsibilities? Who are you responsible to? Your existence, as well as your loss of existence, has an effect on your family, organisation and community. Responsibility can easily be seen as a heavy load preventing one from simply taking off or focusing on self-centred interests. However, the act of carrying this load also sustains life for others. Our role in relation to others around anchors us. My key responsibilities are to my children, parents and the people I work with. What about you?

Ang Peng Siong – Portrait in Anchoring

Let's hear from Uncle Siong, as we call him at the swimming pool, on how these four elements come together for him. He was the world's fastest swimmer in 1982, a managing director of a swimming school and club, former head coach of the Singapore swimming team and now a behind-the-scenes builder of Singapore's sporting culture.

Seated in a meeting room in the swim club with the coaches' sharp whistles and water splashing in the background, I ask

> *"Order is not pressure which is imposed on society from without, but an equilibrium which is set up from within."*
>
> **– Jose Ortega y Gasset**

Uncle Siong, "You have achieved much in your life. How do you see yourself, your identity?"

Uncle Siong is awkwardly silent for a moment, evidence of his self-effacing nature. Searching for the right words, he eventually says, "I would define myself as someone who has found my purpose through sports." As the conversation continues, I find myself learning much more about what it means to be a sportsman than I ever did from the years of dropping my children at the swimming pool.

Uncle Siong has sports in his life. Being an athlete and coach is a pivotal part of his identity. He learnt to swim at the age of five from his father, a pool warden at Farrer Park, and only retired from competitive swimming at 30 years old.

With an unmistakable sense of gratitude, Uncle Siong says, "My father was my first coach and also my inspiration. I remember bringing breakfast to him in the early morning. He would be coaching at the pool at 5.30 a.m. In the evenings, he started his second shift as the coach and president of the Judo Club. Even though we didn't talk much, I saw the years of dedication and the impact he had on the club and the judo players."

In 1982 Uncle Siong was the only non-American to qualify in a major international competition and subsequently became the fastest 50m freestyler in that year. In spite of this, the Olympics medal eluded him. In the 1984 Los Angeles Olympics, there was no 50m freestyle event. In the 1988 Seoul Olympics, while every athlete was training hard, he was in National Service (compulsory military conscription for all Singaporean men). He came ninth in the heats, just one place short of qualifying for the finals. He was so sad that he cried.

"Everything happens for a reason," Uncle Siong quips with a distant look in his eyes. The loss made him committed to developing future athletes and the sports ecosystem. The club played an integral role in promoting paralympics and nurtured swimmers such as Yip Pin Xiu, a world record holder in 100m backstroke.[17] He sees himself as playing a role in influencing the sporting scene in Singapore, so athletes have the support to maximise their window of opportunity into sports at the highest level. This is a responsibility he carries seriously.

"We are here not to create champions but an environment where champions are inevitable," Uncle Siong tells me, repeating the words of Forbes Carlile, Australia's first post-WWII Olympics swimming coach and the only person to have coached and later competed at the Olympic Games. "These words represent the purpose of my work," he says.

In competitive sports, winning a medal is often the final performance indicator. We remember the champion or at best the top three winners, but rarely the others. But Uncle Siong disagrees: "Although not everyone can be an Olympic medallist, we can all be champions in our own life. Our work is to create an environment for everyone to be champions in their own way." A champion trains hard, learns from failure and examines how he or she can do better. Many athletes have gone on to have good careers in their lives. Sports builds their character and habits to be successful in life.

"Sportsmanship is a value we hope to cultivate in our athletes," he tells me. "Sports has the potential to bring people together

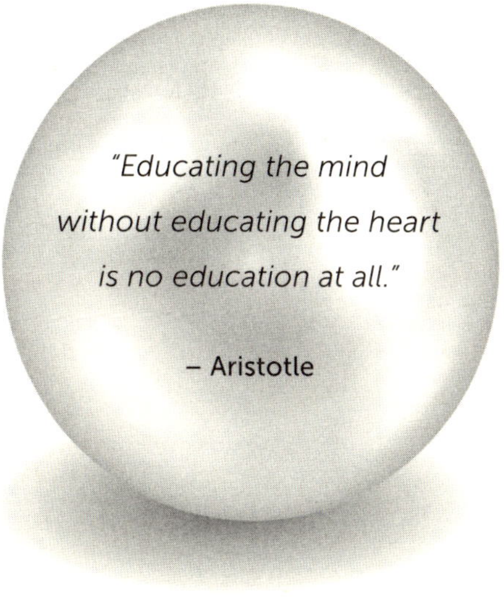

> *"True self is beyond the layers, identities or the hats we wear. We know our true self from its fruits – joy, compassion and wisdom."*
>
> **– Laurence Freeman**

as fellow human beings – to put our differences aside and bring out the best in humankind."

Uncle Siong glances at his watch, a subtle signal that he has to get back to coaching. I thank him and sit a while longer to watch as this tall muscular man returns to the pool deck and shouts, "Go!" and the swimmers plunge into the water in unison. Uncle Siong is an example of wholeness in our anchor, the coming together of one's identity, purpose, responsibility and values, creating congruence and commitment.

Values and purpose have been much talked about; now let's explore identity and responsibilities further. Identity is how we see ourselves, and responsibility is what we are accountable for.

IDENTITY

We tend to define ourselves based on our roles. For example, I am Wendy Tan, founding partner of Flame Centre, a speaker, writer and consultant, Pete's mother, James's daughter, and a Singaporean. My background is in psychology and organisation development. These labels offer familiarity, safety and predictability. But what else lies beyond these externally defined forms of identity?

We do not have to be defined by our body, job title, expertise, affiliations or possessions. Our core identity comes from within. It is deeper and self-constructed. The fruits of our core identity manifest in all aspects of our life. Awareness of our core identity gives us clarity and security from within.

Many years ago, I participated in an expedition to Mongolia with a group of youths from many countries. I was the only Singaporean. No one knew my past and few even knew what or where was Singapore! Away from my familiar environment, I could be whoever I wanted to be and do whatever I wanted to do. Voices of concerned parents, childhood friends, and society norms were far from the scorching sand dunes of the Gobi Desert. Thankfully, there was nothing irresponsible!

The layers of my externally defined identity peeled off gradually, and I experienced an unsettling and uncomfortable void. However, as I connected with the vast expanse of nature, I felt an inner calm develop. I can't say I found my identity on that expedition, but I experienced a quiet sense of freedom in not having a script that I had to follow. I was finally able to hear my inner voice.

Many years later, there have been moments when I felt reconnected with this inner quiet during solitary jogs and while meditating. These moments are liberating because I don't feel beholden to what I'm "supposed to do" as an adult, a mother, a professional or anything else. Without these layers, I have glimpsed my identity in its essence. What I saw was an explorer, someone curious about the world and ideas.

During a Wisdom 2.0 conference in Singapore in 2015, Laurence Freeman, director of The World Community for Christian Meditation, shared a conversation he'd had with the founding prime minister of Singapore, the late Lee Kuan Yew[18]. Mr Lee had said his meditation experience made him aware of an inner self that was more important than the one that the world thought about. To him, the true self is beyond the public self and we

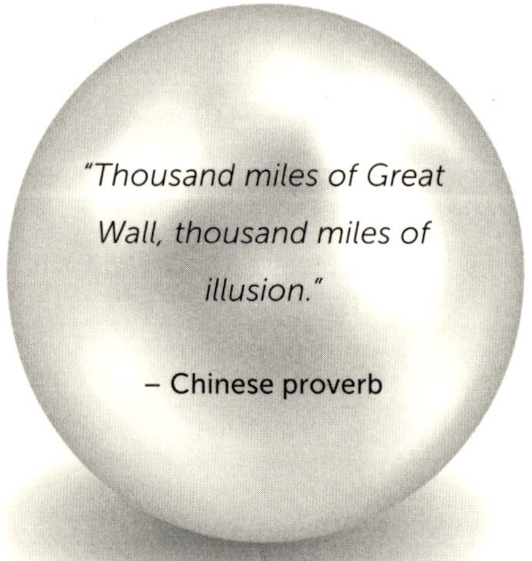

know this true self from its fruits, which include joy, compassion and wisdom.

RESPONSIBILITY

Responsibility seems like a heavy load, the opposite of freedom. For many adults, their children and parents are primary responsibilities. The responsibility I feel towards my own children is enormous.

One evening, when my eldest son was four, the two of us walked past a shop with a fish tank in the window. I noticed one of the goldfish had gone belly-up. I exclaimed, "Oh no, this fish is dying!" My son said gently to the fish, "Don't worry. Mummy is coming." At that moment, I realised the role I play in his life – my job as a mum is to "save" him and support him. It's a sacred responsibility.

Leaders in organisations take responsibility for their subordinates, stakeholders and even the world. Many organisations have corporate social responsibility programmes. Philanthropists such as Bill Gates, Warren Buffett and Li Ka-shing donate to give back to society. Political leaders sign up to be responsible to their constituents and country. Harry Truman was declining in popularity during his presidential term, yet he made decisions to end World War II and abolish racial discrimination in government hiring practices. Lee Kuan Yew saw Singapore as his responsibility and closely guarded its well-being. Nelson Mandela saw as his responsibility the reconciliation of his country.

"Yesterday I was clever, so I wanted to change the world. Today I am wise, so I am changing myself."

– Rumi

Responsibility can feel heavy and stifling. At times we must make choices that curtail our individual freedom. During these moments, it helps to remember that these responsibilities represent our connection to others – our families, organisations and communities. When responsibility is part of our anchor, we become more other-centred, and in our small or big way, create a better world for all. This in turn contributes to our own well-being.

OVER TO YOU

What is your Anchor?

1. The roots of a tree hold it firm. The "roots" for us are our identity, values, responsibility and purpose. Reflect for a moment on these questions:

   a. **Values:** What matters to you? What guides you in making the choices you make?

   b. **Purpose:** What is meaningful to you? What is your purpose?

   c. **Responsibility:** Who or what do you choose to be responsible to?

d. **Identity:** What are the roles in your life? How do you see yourself? Who are you, beyond your professional and family roles?

You can summarise your answers on the tree roots in the illustration below. Download the Anchor Tool fillable PDF from www.wholenessinadisruptiveworld.com for free.

2. Now that you are clearer about your anchor, look at your calendar or reflect on your activities over the past week. To what extent have you spent your time in alignment with your anchor?

   a. What would you want to do more of?

   b. What would you want to do less of?

   c. What do you need to do to shift towards greater alignment between how you spend your time and your anchor?

Now one of your dilemmas could be spending too much time on work. You may feel you do not have a choice in this. Sometimes it is true. Nevertheless, it is possible to have more balance. It is okay if you do not have all the answers immediately. We are only on the first pathway. Let's move on to B – Balancing.

CHAPTER 5
BALANCING

To yield is to be preserved whole.
To be bent is to become straight.
To be hollow is to be filled.
To be tattered is to be renewed.
To be in want is to possess.
To have plenty is to be confused.
Therefore the Sage embraces the One.
– *Dao De Jing*, Chapter 22

The second element of the ABCs of wholeness is balancing. Is balance like a weighing scale that when one side is up, the other side is necessarily down? So when one party wins, the other party loses? Or is balance a 50:50 compromise? You win some and I win some?

I don't believe so. If you push your palms against each other with equal force, what do you get? A stalemate despite a lot of energy expended. So balance is not 50:50. Rather, to balance we need to first get *out of* balance. I learnt this from *taiji*. To move, we need to shift our weight, 70 percent then eventually 100 percent on one foot, while we lift the other foot. At this point, we are out of balance, and we shift our weight to the other foot again to regain balance. The continuous being out of balance and then rebalancing results in movement and energy flow. This is dynamic balance, so we get 100:100 over time. It is not "either-or", but "and". The alternating of the opposites over time creates an output that is more expansive and life-sustaining. So balancing is embracing opposites 100:100 over time to give us cognitive wholeness.

Let's see what this means at work.

Susan Chong – Balancing opposites creatively

Susan is a mother of four and founder of Greenpac, a market leader in innovative green packaging solutions. I asked her, "What helped you and Greenpac be successful?"

"Packaging is all about customising solutions to meet customers' needs," she responds in a matter-of-fact way, explaining that manufacturers usually have to choose between using cheaper plastic materials and using more expensive recycled ones. "Everyone says it's great to have green solutions, but they refuse to pay more for it. Whatever we do has to make economic sense."

To be green and cost-effective, Greenpac redesigns both the physical packages and the packing process. For example, Greenpac uses less foam in a Leica microscope storage box and thus saves 25 percent on packaging costs. Rather than accept either-or solutions for her clients' packaging needs, Susan seeks creative solutions which are both environmentally friendly and cost-efficient.

"In our business, it's not just about low prices. Long-term partnerships with suppliers and customers make the difference. During the 2008 financial crisis, one of our suppliers could not honour the contracted price as their margins were severely eroded. Rather than shop for another low-price supplier, we worked together with them to find a solution." They pored over different designs, materials and manufacturing processes to find viable options. Consequently, trust was deepened and the supplier has delivered ever since. "Today, Greenpac has an edge

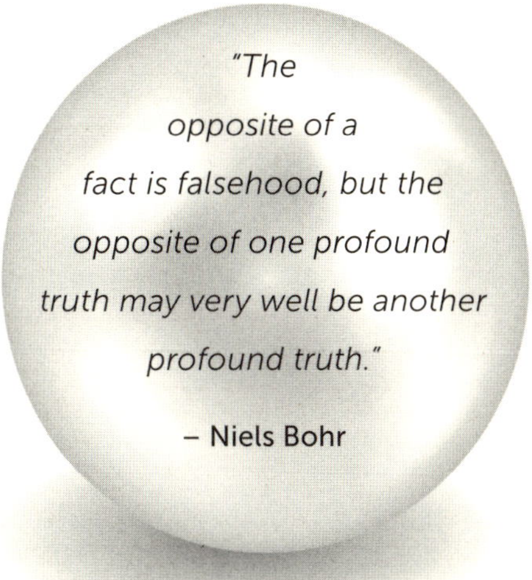

because it integrates knowledge from a variety of long-term suppliers."

Greenpac also builds long-term partnerships with its employees. "We work like a family. Each staff member is like an arm or a leg, and the company cannot function without any one part." Being a lean company with a flat hierarchy, they cook lunch together in the office's state-of-the-art kitchen using the hydroponic vegetables from the office garden.

Just as Susan develops partnerships and relationships – the *yin*, or softer aspect of the business – she is equally comfortable taking a hard-nosed approach to her business with her practical in-depth knowledge of the industry.

Susan laughs as she recounts how she once welcomed two Japanese clients, who started the meeting with, "Can we meet

> *"I've learned that you can't have everything and do everything at the same time."*
>
> **– Oprah Winfrey**

your boss?" To which she replied, "I am the boss." Both gentlemen tried to hide their surprise, rather unsuccessfully. They remained skeptical until in the course of the meeting they realised she knew the business inside out. Susan keeps her business perspectives and management acumen sharp by continuing to educate herself. The two clients left the meeting satisfied.

Susan's skill in bringing opposites together – low-cost and green, business and relationship – brings about an outcome that's superior to either-or solutions. She exemplifies how balancing opposites can help us creatively deal with challenges.

WHAT IS BALANCING OPPOSITES?

Although *yin-yang* philosophy is a commonly known ancient concept, it has subtle insights that are worth further reflection. *Yin-yang* informs us how to recognise polarities and to observe the way they change over time to create a thirdness in the process. According to Robin Wang, author of *Yinyang: The Way of Heaven and Earth in Chinese Thought and Culture*[19], *yin-yang* philosophy has four elements:

- Contradictory interdependence
- Mutual inclusion
- Complementary support
- Thirdness

> *"The end is the beginning of all things, suppressed and hidden, awaiting to be released through the rhythm of pain and pleasure."*
>
> – Jiddu Krishnamurti

Contradictory interdependence (矛盾而相依, *mao dun er xiang yi*). The basis of any *yin-yang* distinction is tension between the two sides that allows dynamic creation to come through their interaction. The day-night cycle beautifully illustrates this. Other polarities include sun vs. moon, masculine vs. feminine and East vs. West. In the work context, some polarities are business vs. relationships, short vs. long term, strategy vs. implementation, opportunities vs. risk. Polarities exist in every situation. What polarities do you encounter?

Mutual inclusion (互含, *hu han*). This means one force is contained within the other. Among the seasons, summer, being the warmest, is considered the most *yang*, yet it also contains a *yin* force that begins to emerge in the summer, extends through fall, and reaches its culmination in the winter. Winter, being the coldest, is the highest stage of *yin*, yet a *yang* force within it unfolds through spring and attains full strength in summer.

Years ago, my former managing director, Kay Yong, said, "The best time to change is when we are strong." We were a pharmaceutical company, and had several years of being the "jewel" in the manufacturing network, with high product quality and yield with relatively low cost. Everyone thought we were in a good place. But he continued to champion change relentlessly. Being "better, cheaper and faster" was the focus of the change efforts.

Late one evening, Kay Yong came "managing by walking around". Most of the staff had left already. As a relatively new, young (and politically naïve) internal organisation development consultant, I blurted out to him, "Why do we, hmm, actually why do *you* drive change so relentlessly?" I felt silly once the words came out, though this question was common corridor talk. His gaze pierced through me, as if I should know the answer, and he replied with a stately air, "What we see is the site doing well, what we don't see are the risks on the horizon." He went on to share about the push for automation; the risks to the livelihood of the production workers if they didn't upskill; and the need to add more value to the network by being a product innovation site rather than simply manufacturing to specifications. These projections were three to four years away. "When we are strong, we need to prepare for the unseen forces that will manifest in time. Now we have time. Time is opportunity." I left the office that day thinking, "Wow, this is foresight."

While one force is at full strength, another force waits in the background and will manifest in time. With the polarity you have in mind, which is in the foreground, which is in the background? What is seen, what is unseen?

Complementary support (互补, *hu bu*). This means each side supplies what the other lacks. This does not mean one submits to the other, because both sides stand on equal ground in performing different roles. We tend to lean toward logical decision-making, business focus and scientific achievements and downplay the role of the opposing polarity. But logic-intuition, business-relationships and science-arts, just to name a few, stand on equal ground and support each other.

Similarly there are a few Western thinkers who speak about embracing polarities. F. Scott Fitzgerald famously said, "The test of first-rate intelligence is the ability to hold two opposed ideas in the mind at the same time, and still retain the ability to function"[20]. The poet Walt Whitman also asked in his poem, "Song to Myself":

> *Do I contradict myself?*
> *Very well then I contradict myself.*
> *I am large,*
> *I contain multitudes.*[21]

What do these ideas mean in everyday life? Business meetings offer a great example of how these polarities can make for effective management. Referring to how to close out a meeting of an executive team that we were facilitating together, my mentor, Peter Block, asked, "What is needed for them to be whole?" Great meetings are those that take care of tasks and deepen relationships. They clarify strategy and inspire commitment.

Wholeness in meetings is an expression of opposing and complementary polarities: task + relationship; action + reflection; divergence + convergence; performance + spirit.

Many meetings focus on tasks and leave connection and commitment to chance. A whole meeting focuses on both *what* and *how*, e.g., what is the work to be done and how do we be with one another. In essence, it is both doing and being. We attend to the work to be done and deepen relationships as well. It has space for both action and reflection. It allows for divergence of ideas before convergence of decisions. Within this is active agreeing and disagreeing. It is the essence of a high-performing team.

In the polarity you have in mind, how do they support each other? Think of examples from your life.

Thirdness. *Yin* and *yang* are really a form of triadic thinking centred on polarity interaction. The continuous shifting of *yin* and *yang* over time gives us seasons, day and night – the rhythm of life. This is the thirdness created. It is also expansive and life-giving. Similarly, breathing in and out gives us energy, the thirdness created.

The thirdness created from whole meetings is a sense of engagement, empowerment and enablement. In the manufacturing example above, Kay Yong was creating a series of S-curve growths by working with seen and unseen forces. Susan's thirdness is a sustainable business model. Similarly, alternating work and personal life creates work-life integration. Focusing on business and relationships brings about viable partnerships. Focusing on I and we creates sustainable communities.

What thirdness is created from the polarities you deal with?

DYNAMIC BALANCE HAPPENS OVER TIME

Laura Hsu, a master facilitator based in Taiwan, uses the four seasons and farming as a metaphor to suggest that changing priorities and actions in different contexts enables sustainable results. In spring, farmers plough; in summer, they weed; in autumn, they harvest; and in winter, they store away the grain. When these are attended to in the right order, the grains will be replenished cyclically, and an abundant supply of food is guaranteed.[22] This thinking acknowledges there is a time for everything.

The question is, when is it time for *what*? Answering that requires wisdom. As we become aware of our habits and explore alternatives, we can intentionally shift our thinking and our life towards wholeness. How does this idea apply to everyday life? As I was recovering from my illness, I wondered if I should stop work and spend time with my children. So my thinking was either career or family. But this was not a satisfying compromise, not to mention that my tiger mum instincts would have driven the family up the wall! I wanted to have my cake and eat it too. What good is a cake if we can't eat it?

My insight was this idea of dynamic balance – the interplay of opposites over time. When I am at work, writing or travelling, I am 100 percent at it. When I am with my children, helping them with their work or music, I am 100 percent at it. I am 100:100 at both, and over time I integrate both work and family to create a life I love. It does require more creativity to find better ways of doing things, a network of support at work and home, and clarity on what I want and what I say "no" to.

Two women, Shirley and Tina, gave me faith that wholeness as a career mum is possible. Both eventually retired at the top of their organisations. They had shifted to part-time work when their children were young and were glad they'd spent time with their children when they needed their mothers most and felt good about contributing to their development. Even when their careers were in low gear, these women continued to sharpen themselves. When the time was right to re-engage at work, they didn't shy away from bigger roles.

Similarly, Sumit, a participant in one of my workshops, is a brilliant engineer and valued for his technical prowess. However, the non-linear messy world of relationships and political dynamics frustrated him. After some failures, he understood that if he wanted to be successful, he needed to open himself to new and unfamiliar ways of approaching work. He developed his skills in personnel management and learned to engage people through cooperation, inspiration and alliance-building. The interplay of technical knowledge and interpersonal understanding helped Sumit become more effective in his work. He embraced cognitive wholeness and acquired both technical and interpersonal skills in the process.

Wholeness in our thinking helps us see things from different perspectives and appreciate the strength or truth in each. It's even more relevant today than in the past as people from different cultural backgrounds work together. Conflicts stem from single-truth viewpoints that pigeonhole people as right or wrong, good or evil and promote an "us against them" mentality. This results in much of the fragmentation and fundamentalism we see in the world today.

CHALLENGES TO COGNITIVE WHOLENESS

Unfortunately, in many ways, our thinking is conditioned by our culture, upbringing and education, combined with our own inborn nature. Early on, we develop mental models that determine not only what we see but our willingness and capacity to see. Using their proprietary Leadership Versatility Index to evaluate 7,000 managers and CEOs, Kaplan and Kaiser noted in *Fear Your Strengths*[23] that many had negative relationships between their strengths and weaknesses.[24] This means leaders strong in one quality had a 90 percent chance of being rated as lacking in equal but opposite skills. For example, a forceful leader was

> *"A self is not something static, tied up in a pretty parcel and handed to the child, finished and complete. A self is always becoming."*
>
> – **Madeleine L'Engle**

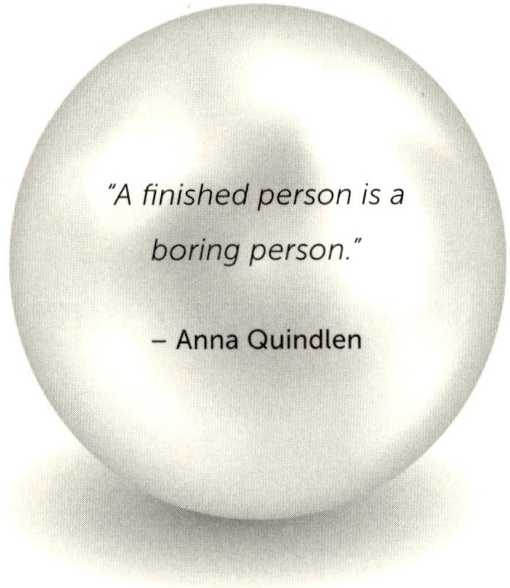

unlikely to be rated as having an enabling style, and a strategic leader was unlikely to be rated highly in operational functions.

The authors offered numerous examples of how overused strengths (that is, too much weight on one polarity) eventually led to failure, and they emphasised the need to be both – strategic and operational, forceful and enabling. In their book, they acknowledged that many leaders experienced the opposing characteristics as dissonance robbing them of their distinctiveness instead of as complementary forces suggested by the *yin-yang* philosophy. However, Kaplan and Kaiser noted that the key lies in versatility and knowing what behaviour is appropriate in each situation.

Interestingly, only about 10 percent of the 7,000 leaders studied had profiles that showed versatility. Versatile leaders have an ability to tune in to the workplace situation, identify the needs of the situation and the people involved. If leaders are distracted by their ego needs, such as wondering what people will think of them, they tend to be less effective.

Here's another barrier to cognitive wholeness. Modern education teaches students to categorise and think using models. In fact, the word "science" originally meant separate. Early in life, we are trained to analyse characteristics and separate them into categories, thereby finding order in chaos. This categorical thinking leads to either-or patterns and we tend to dismiss more inclusive way of thinking.

To make knowledge simple and accessible, we develop paradigms for everything – leadership, strategic formulation, implementation, development, finance, marketing and so on. In fact, we think using models, and then we try to fit what we experience into predesignated categories. While such templates make knowledge neat and easy to understand, they also remove subtle options that can lead to deeper principles or philosophical approaches to problem solving. For example, the McKinsey Seven-S Framework[25] identifies how to set up an organisation, but it doesn't address how it could work in tandem with the changing environment.

This linear, analytical and logical-thinking approach comes more from the Western tradition than Eastern. Eastern thinking tends to be conveyed through stories, abstract phrases, principles and metaphors. The *Dao De Jing*[26], for example, is a short text with 81 brief chapters and 5,000 Chinese characters that offers singular ideas written in poetic sentences. These texts use short, declarative statements with intentional contradictions. The first of these strategies creates memorable phrases, while the second forces us to somehow reconcile the supposed contradictions. In this way, the meaning is open to interpretation and only accessible after discussion and reflection.

IS DYNAMIC BALANCE A CONVENIENT COMPROMISE?

When I shared this idea of embracing opposites with colleagues, they pointed out that embracing "and" in our thinking seems to be uninteresting or lacking in conviction. They believed that one should take a stand, and moreover, the more radical the stand, the more interesting or valuable it is.

Perhaps this disdain comes from categorical thinking itself – this or that, yes or no, black or white, opposition or proposition. Since Socrates' day, debating has been the test of the rigour of one's thinking. There is a win/lose position. But either-or positions polarise issues and put people in different camps – e.g., liberals vs. conservatives, haves and have-nots. We get stuck in repetitive loops of ideology and think, "I'm right, you're wrong". Is this useful for individual or community wholeness?

Embracing opposites is not a middle-of-the-road compromise. It is flexing our thinking to find the creative thirdness that honours both perspectives, guided by our anchor – our values, identity, purpose and responsibility. Just as a strong spine enables our body to both be erect and bend in different positions,

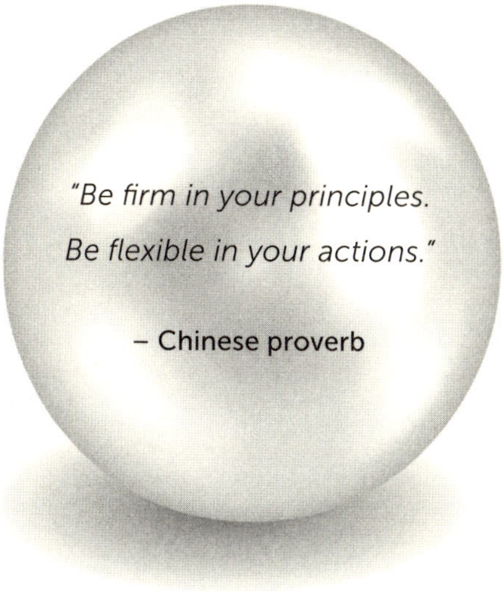

a strong anchor permits us to stand firm on our values but be flexible in our execution.

Ancient Chinese coins were typically round with a square hole in the middle (外圆内方, *wai yuan nei fang*). We can interpret this as being sharp on our principles internally but smooth and non-offensive in implementation or external manifestation.

There are few absolute truths in the world, but one of these truths is that humans can be angels or devils. A Cherokee elder sitting with his grandchildren told them, "In every life, there is a terrible fight – a fight between two wolves. One is evil: he is fear, anger, envy, greed, arrogance, self-pity, resentment and deceit. The other is good: joy, serenity, humility, confidence, generosity, truth, gentleness and compassion." A child asked, "Grandfather, which wolf will win?" The elder looked at him in the eye and replied, "The one you feed."

We all experience both selfish and selfless thoughts, and thankfully, we can choose which voice to listen to. Given these differences in human motivations, is there a place for deploying both care and fear tactics? I love my children and also threaten them when they choose to behave in dangerous, destructive or lazy ways.

Choosing to manage through both care and fear is a tactic based on our anchor – love and sense of responsibility towards our loved ones, staff and country. This anchor stays constant, even if we choose to use fear as a tactic. We do it because it serves a larger purpose, the collective. In this sense, there is no fixed ideology; instead, embracing opposites is guided by our anchor, just as our flexible body is supported by our straight spine.

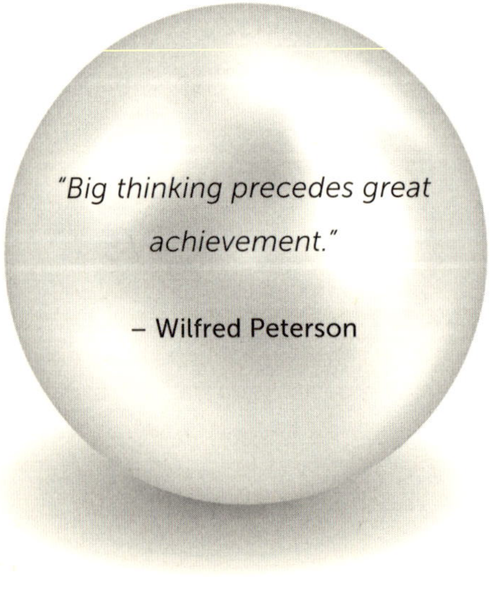

HOW TO HAVE MORE COGNITIVE WHOLENESS

While culture undoubtedly influences habits, Richard Nisbett[27] points out that people are capable of broadening their views. Here are some suggestions.

First, resist accepting the either-or, trade-off mentality. Don't buy into the conventional saying that we cannot have our cake and eat it too. Don't believe that we need to trade our personal lives for our careers or that we cannot take care of both relationships and work or any other polarities.

Many years ago, I had an argument with my professor. He said we couldn't have high-quality and cost-effective goods. It's true that some cheap goods are lousy, and some expensive goods are high-quality. But there are goods that are both high-quality and cost-effective. It's more empowering to say "I don't know how" and search for the answers than assume it is impossible.

In a similar vein, do not accept solutions that force a compromise. Strive for perfect solutions. Obviously, we cannot always have immediate perfect solutions, but we can have them *over time*. Here's an example. A technical engineer at a pharmaceutical company lamented, "Every time we ask Compliance if we can simplify the process, they say no and cite regulatory requirements as the reason. It's quite discouraging." On the other hand, a Compliance officer said, "Product Development tries to simplify, but that's really cutting corners. People don't understand that controls are there for a reason." Does this sound familiar?

Innovation is a struggle and tension rises between the two departments.

The clash between quality compliance and innovation is an eternal one. Procedures, processes and controls are necessary to ensure quality and safe products. Safeguards protect the interests of the organisation and its customers. The result? Compliance polices adherence. They demand multiple levels of approvals. They threaten to audit you. On the other hand, innovation results in new products and simplified processes needed for company growth and lower costs. Innovation requires freedom. Simple fast processes. Access to technology. Willingness to take risks.

How can we resolve this conflict? Ong Boon Kee, a regional quality director at GlaxoSmithKline, describes how they do it. "It's looking enterprise-wide, beyond individual functions, to recognise our common purpose (anchor)," he says. People often forget that both the smaller units and the company as a whole have the common objective of serving the customers. "If you're the patient, what kind of medicine would you want?" Clearly, everyone wants effective, safe and affordable medicine.

How could these departments work together to be both innovative and compliant? Boon Kee explains simply, "When both departments agree on the same desired outcome, we then agree on the problem statement." What appears to be a problem to Compliance may not seem important to Product Development, and this is why disagreements arise. When everyone agrees to the problem statement, both parties can work toward identifying the "third ways". These are the critical steps and control points that need to be incorporated into the process so the eventual output is both innovative and compliant. As an example, both departments agree to buy raw materials at the right cost and quality.

Boon Kee adds, "Because Product Development faces time pressure to launch new products quickly and cost efficiently, Compliance needs to be engaged early in the process so the quality requirements can be taken into consideration. In this process, both parties understand the mutual perspectives, e.g., why a particular process is necessary or examine assumptions for keeping a process. They are creative, whilst keeping to compliance requirements."

So to cultivate cognitive wholeness, we first need to identify the polarities in the situation. See these polarities as complementary,

mutually inclusive, and standing on equal ground but playing different roles. Some examples of polarities include I and we, task and relationships, career and personal life, short and long term, care and discipline. Then take guidance from your anchor – what are your values, purpose, responsibilities and identity? Consider what is the larger thirdness possible in these situations? Identify creative options that embrace inclusive solutions instead of either-or compromises. Manage constraints such as time, money, resources and energy. Give space for the solution to develop, knowing that wholeness is achieved over time.

OVER TO YOU

Gaining Mobius Insight™

If you are facing a dilemma or a challenging situation, use these questions to find some new perspectives:

1. What is this situation about?

2. What are the polarities involved in this situation?

   Pole A:

   Pole B:

3. What is your anchor? What is the wholeness you are seeking?

4. What are the *negative* behaviours associated with each polarity?

Negative Behaviours

Pole A	Pole B

5. What are the *positive* behaviours associated with each polarity?

Positive Behaviours

Pole A	Pole B

6. Look at the list of *positive* behaviours under each pole. Can you engage in both behaviours? What are some creative and innovative options?

7. What insights come to you? What is cognitive wholeness in this situation?

For the full version of the Mobius Insight™ Tool, visit our website at www.wholenessinadisruptiveworld.com.

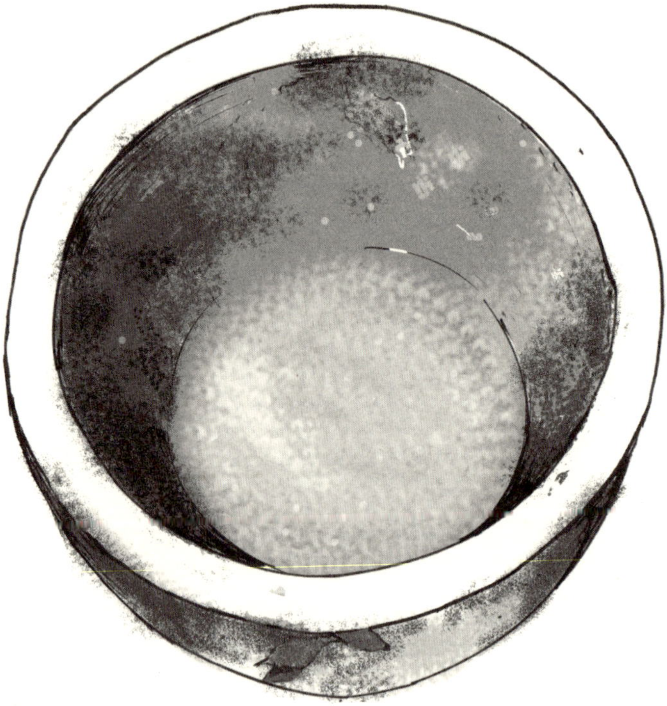

CHAPTER 6
CLEARING

Mould clay into a vessel;
From its not-being (in the vessel's hollow)
Arises the utility of the vessel.
By the existence of things, we profit.
And by the non-existence of things, we are served.
– *Dao De Jing*, Chapter 11

Clearing is emptying our mental clutter, judgments and emotions, and being whole in the moment. When we empty out, there is a void. In nothingness, we just be and are whole in the moment. This void allows us to receive new ideas and connect to when, who and what matters.

Kevin Cashman, author of *Leadership from Inside Out*, writes that we need to pause and reflect in the midst of the pace and complexity of the environments we operate in. After all, moving quickly in the wrong direction won't lead to success. He calls this the ability to be in the "eye of the hurricane of life". This gives a glimpse of clearing to be whole in the moment.[28]

How does this concept apply in the workplace? Lim Boon Huat is the managing director of the Asia branch of Rohde and Schwarz, the world's leading supplier of wireless communications equipment. With a PhD in management and background in engineering, he has led the growth of his company from a 15-person outfit to one with more than 350 employees. When I ask him about applying the concept of clearing, he brings up his motivational speech at the company's annual meeting.

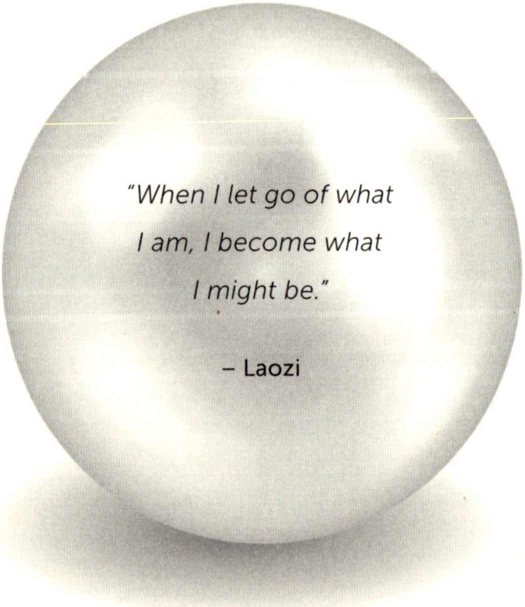

"When I am addressing my staff, this process is like a dance between me and them," he says. "Of course, before the meeting, I prepare by going through the objectives, business context, key messages, talking points, examples and stories." He works out the flow of how one idea links to another and rehearses his delivery. I ask, "So these are all action-oriented 'doing' activities?" He nods in agreement.

"However, just before going up to the podium, I take several deep breaths. I relax and let go of the need to memorise the script. It's like emptying myself. This also means trusting myself to go with the flow. I remind myself to look at my people and sense their emotions." Boon Huat is whole in the moment. Rather than recite his speech monotonously, as what some leaders and politicians do, he allows himself to connect with his audience, go with the flow and *be* his speech.

PURPOSEFUL NON-DOING

The *Dao De Jing*, a pivotal work on Chinese thought, discusses 无为 (*wu wei*), or non-action. This non-doing is not being idle or lazy but advocates purposeful observation and a flow that synchronises with unfolding events. This is because *dao* does not struggle; it lets things unfold by themselves according to the right time in nature. The idea is not to force things to happen but to seize opportunities when they arise. This notion of non-doing contrasts with busy doing:

Busy Doing	Purposeful Non-doing
Squeezing in an email reply at the red light while driving.	Noticing the surroundings or listening to your passenger.
Many simultaneous thoughts and a compulsion to record them lest they are lost.	Nothing in particular on one's mind. Observing thoughts coming in and slipping away.
Hassled, hurried, distracted and impatient.	Calm and at peace.
Unaware of or lacking intention.	Connected with one's anchor.
Multi-tasking, trying to do several things at the same time.	Focus is on one thing at a time.
Focus on oneself. Too distracted to listen to and focus on others.	Connect with the people in your presence, aware of their spoken and unspoken needs.
Preoccupied with the past or future.	Present in the moment.
Expend a great deal of effort. Restless energy.	Restful and allow things to take place easily.
Attempt to control the process.	Comfortable letting the process unfold.
Experience of time is limited or hurried.	Experience of time expands.

WHY CLEARING IS IMPORTANT

A disciple visited the Zen master and asked him, "What more can I learn from you, Teacher?" The master began to pour the student a cup of tea. The cup filled, but the teacher continued to pour, and the cup overflowed. Surprised, the disciple shouted, "Stop! It's full already! Why do you keep pouring?" The Zen master looked at the young man and said, "If your mind is already full, how can you take in any more?" The disciple realised his arrogance and learned about the need to be empty. Clearing is needed for a few reasons.

Unlearning and living a different today from yesterday. I asked a senior manager how he was applying the learning after a training workshop. His reply, "Well, I've been busy and now many people are on leave. I am waiting for a good opportunity to apply the new skills." I asked him, "Will there be a time you're not

busy? Will there be a perfect opportunity to apply the learning?" Probably not. Has he learnt from the workshop? Probably not. Living our life in auto-pilot mode and repeating the same routine gives us more of yesterday. Unlearning requires us to take time to jump out of this auto-pilot mode and intentionally take new actions.

Access to new ideas. When someone asked the great composer J.S. Bach how he came up with his melodies, he said, "The problem is not finding them, it's when getting up in the morning and getting out of bed, not stepping on them."[29] When we are empty, fresh ideas – like new melodies – creep into our consciousness. In this state, the internal chatter is silent and we are empty to receive. Ideas flow in effortlessly.

You may have experienced situations in which new ideas, connections or perspectives come to you unexpectedly. This can happen when you exercise, play music, shower, meditate or simply go for a stroll. What's common to these activities? There is no deliberate effort to brainstorm for answers; they just come when we empty our mind and be in the moment. When I jog or meditate in the mornings, sometimes ideas and insights drop into my consciousness that prompt me to spend my day differently.

Mastery over context and choice. When we clear our mind, we connect to the present moment and sense the context and what might be emerging. We become aware of met or unmet needs, and we see people as they are without being judgmental or labelling them. Our subsequent actions are more deliberate and productive. For example, to manage a rude or difficult employee, a leader might decide to raise his voice not in knee-jerk anger but in an intentional manner to gain control. If the leader had not raised his voice, the employee might have a negative impact on the team dynamics. The idea is to choose the response instead of reacting impulsively. Thus, in the moment, we take advantage of the opportunity to switch from an automatic reaction to an intentional and conscious response.

When we have a difficult conversation with a non-performing subordinate, emptying ourselves of our judgments and negative emotions helps us realise that our opinion is only one perspective and not the absolute truth. This leads us to be more open to other perspectives, increasing the likelihood that the conversation will be productive and beneficial.[30]

This is similar to the notion of mindfulness. Ellen Langer, a

Harvard professor widely acknowledged as the mother of mindfulness, defines it as "a process of perceiving changes in a given context and noticing what is new. When you do that, it puts you in the present."[31] It involves attending to what is novel and actively making choices. As Langer says, "When you're mindful, rules, routines, and goals guide you; they don't govern you."[32] The context has changed, but learned behaviour typically does not.

For example, I have worked with some trainers who are used to delivering training in a fire-hose style and "downloading" concepts to learners. However, today's context has changed. The younger workforce learns in a different way. Knowledge is easily found on the internet, so learners can Google the information when needed and don't feel the need to remember the information. Under the illusion that they "know" already, they tend not to focus on acquiring skills or developing the finer judgment required to do their job well.

To be effective in this new context, trainers need to clear or erase their old ways of teaching content and help learners first realise their "illusion of knowing", then challenge them with tasks or projects and let them discover their shortcomings themselves. Or they could facilitate discussions to help learners articulate and examine their assumptions. All these activities are more challenging and require more skills from the trainers than the lecture approach.

Mastering context and choice means that our understanding of the larger system guides our actions. Learning from the feedback of our actions, we take action again. This is like trimming our sails according to the wind, instead of keeping to the pre-determined course or acting mindlessly within our conditioned modes of thinking.[33] This conscious way of operating is key in today's accelerating rate of change and the disruptive world. Observing subtle differences in the moment helps us to anticipate how things might turn out and to be prepared to manage the future rather than be managed by it.

Focus on the right actions for the longer term. Clearing our negative emotions such as anxiety within ourselves also builds patience and our capacity for growth. There is a Chinese story about a farmer who pulled his seedlings a bit every day, thinking he was helping them grow faster. Naturally, several days later, his plants died. Instead of letting the plants take their natural course, he tried to force growth to happen, and his impatience and anxiety eventually led to their premature death.

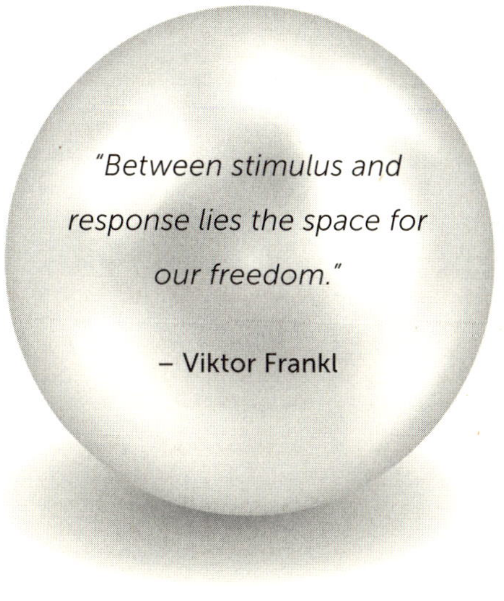

We cannot literally see our children or business grow either, but we know they do. Growth takes time and can be hard to recognise. Therefore, we need to be patient and deal with our anxiety in the process. Being whole even when our work is not complete is a natural state. This doesn't mean we should be complacent; instead, we seek the wisdom to know when to take action and when not to, avoiding the temptation to hot-house our children or take shortcuts in business that inhibit long-term growth.

Building an organisational culture, nurturing the talent pool, increasing customer loyalty – all these things take time. Investing time and patience will provide benefits that far exceed those attained through short-term tactics such as importing ready talent or gaining customers by giving discounts. I worked with a regional sales director in a contact lens business division in a Fortune 500 company. He was dismayed to learn that his sales managers had propped up the year-end numbers by

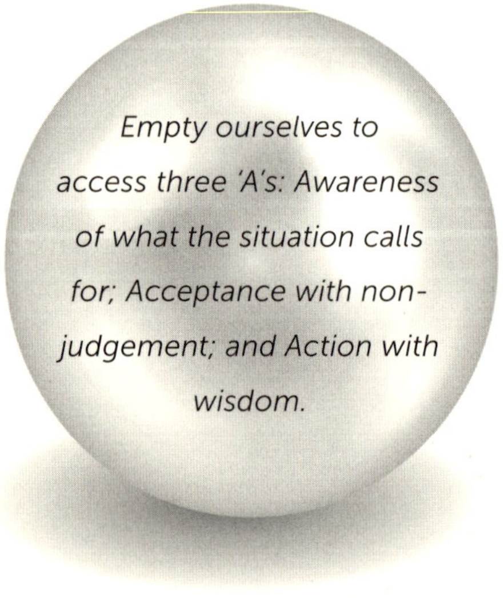

incentivising customers, the optical shops, to stock up. With excess inventory, they naturally did not order for the next two quarters. A better alternative would have been to work with the opticians to educate consumers on the benefits of the superior product or create loyalty programmes to increase long-term sales.

Similarly, with children, we can help them in the longer term by nurturing good habits and character traits such as curiosity, ownership and determination, rather than fill their time with classes. For example, it seems counter-productive to get tuition teachers to drill them to score in examinations, only for them to forget almost everything after that, or to pressure or bribe them to excel in sports and music. Relying on extrinsic motivators squeezes out the cultivation of internal drive.

My nine-year-old son Finn whines, "You must buy me gems (for computer games), then I will continue with the next level in electone class." I reply, "Then you're doing it for the wrong reason. What do you want for yourself in music?" He pauses, refusing to fall for my trick and continues, "You can just encourage me, right?" I just smile. I haven't caved in (yet), but knowing how creative Finn is in getting what he wants, he will probably get the gems from his father! Nevertheless, a more durable approach is to cultivate intrinsic motivation.

Ultimately, we are not "human doings" designed to be busy and distracted as we spend our days ticking items off the "to do" list. Instead, we can think about the term "human being" in this way: We are centred and focused in the moment, connected to ourselves, to what we are doing, and to the people we are with. Whether we are in a meeting with colleagues, preparing a presentation or having dinner with our family, we are whole in the moment. Even if we are not fully accomplished, complete or satisfied, we can still be whole in the moment.

WHY IS IT HARD TO CLEAR AND JUST BE

For a person who lives under the pressure (and pleasure) of completing a "to do" list, purposeful non-doing is tough. Not long before my potentially fatal illness, I visited my geomancer, Lek, who practises *fengshui* and foretells one's life by looking at patterns on the palm, facial features and star signs. At his home office, Lek asked for my date and time of birth. "You are married with three children, right?" he asked, demonstrating his credibility. He made some forecasts about my family, career, wealth and health. Then he paused, looked at me in the eye and said with a more serious tone, "I need to advise you to relax. Having too much *yang* energy will affect your health and family relationships." *Yang* refers to masculine energy – ambitious, fast-paced, impatient and quick-tempered. He was referring to the stress typically experienced by Type A personalities.

While I took his words with a pinch of salt, he was right that I really didn't know how to relax. My every action or task was oriented towards achieving a goal. At work, my team would meet for 30 minutes to strategise and talk about who would do what and when. My life was governed by objectives complete with specific targets and action steps. I was impatient with

"The heart of the wise man lies quiet like limpid water."

– Cameroonian proverb

people who took a long time to express their thoughts and had a disdain for circular discussions. I exercised in the gym to burn calories and build muscle. I measured my distance, time, heart rate and calories burned. Even working with my children was task-oriented. I told them to read a book and underline the new words, practise their music, do their homework and play without quarrelling. You can see why my life broke down.

Emphasis on actions. In our action-oriented and outcome-driven culture, we emphasise acquiring knowledge and working hard to achieve our goals in a competitive environment. Promises of shortcuts to success are everywhere. We have five steps, seven habits, and ten top tips for any area of life we want to improve. We love simple and practical steps because we believe we can achieve what we want by quickly taking easy actions. Emphasising speed and efficiency, we think we can stay focused, perform effectively and achieve our objectives.

Yet before we fully integrate these ideas as part of our being, our fragmented thoughts push us to move on to the next sure-win programme.

What's missing? We often don't take time to deeply consider the underlying values and strategies of the models we attempt to use to improve our lives. Our perpetual fixation on "doing" reinforces our assumption that inaction is not an option. Taking a break, strolling in the garden or taking time to reflect are not considered productive. Even yoga, traditionally a relaxing and healing meditative art has evolved into heart-pumping and fat-burning routines with core, power and hot routines. We are typically not used to slowing down and tapping into our inner wisdom. Yet this purposeful non-doing is exactly what's needed for us to reinvent, relearn and rejuvenate ourselves in this disruptive world.

The message here is not to discount actions or goals but to focus on meaningful actions that come from clarity. Chapter 15 of the *Dao De Jing* describes this alternation of being and doing:

> *Who can find repose in a muddy world?*
> *By lying still, it becomes clear.*
> *Who can maintain his calm for long?*
> *By activity, it comes back to life.*

Negative emotions. Anyone who has felt angry, sad or disappointed knows that negative emotions can grip us powerfully. Instead of clearing and connecting to the present or our anchor, we stew on what's upsetting us and demonise ourselves or the other people involved. Here's an example.

On one occasion, I was angry with my husband for contradicting me in front of my son, Pete, when I was coaching him in his schoolwork. I had asked Pete to do one more task before going to a party, but my husband wanted to give him a break. Due to my husband's interference, Pete didn't complete the task I'd assigned. In my anger, I could neither connect to my anchor as a mother nor be present in the moment. I was hurt that the time and effort I'd invested helping him prepare for his test weren't appreciated. Feeling wronged, I adamantly told myself that I would not help him with his work anymore, and we would see the result. Yes, negative emotions!

A cold war ensued. As the party was by the beach, we walked along the pathway. My younger children, Finn and Sophie, oblivious to the undercurrents, laughed and walked with my husband. Pete trailed some 25 metres behind. I sulkily dragged my feet way behind. The waves were lapping at the shore. A breeze, finally cool during the evening, was blowing lightly. I took a few deep breaths as I tried to reconnect with my anchor. What do I want for myself, Pete and my family? What are my values and responsibilities?

Hearing Sophie's infectious laughter from a distance, I realised that more than being right, I wanted the family to be happy together. Pete sheepishly glanced back to see where I was. I knew he was a sensitive boy and sensed my anger. Slowly the negative emotions dissipated. Thirty minutes later, while the children were in the laser tag party, I initiated a conversation with my husband. Our conversation helped me let go and be present again. Clarity of my anchor, taking time to clear and then rebalancing helped me be the person I wanted to be.

"To be angry with the right person, to the right degree, at the right time, for the right purpose, and in the right way is not easy."

– Aristotle

HOW TO CLEAR AND JUST BE

Wholeness in the moment involves emptying one's mind rather than being distracted by one's emotions and thoughts. Here are some suggestions for how to clear and just be:

Know what is ultimately important. Don't worry about things that don't matter. Marshall Goldsmith, an executive coach and business thinker, says, "Let it go", exhaling and waving his hand in the air. He refers to winning the big ones and letting go of issues that are not worth our time and energy.

Focus on what is ultimately important. In a work context, creating value and serving clients' needs is what sustains a business, not pushing numbers. Nurturing people to learn and take ownership sustains performance, not micromanaging to make sure everything goes according to plan. At home, cultivating a child's interests, ownership and confidence builds a foundation that's more important than getting every worksheet correct or piano piece perfect. Knowing what's ultimately important helps us be more mindful and patient.

Learn the process of emptying. As we finish one activity and before we move on to the next, clearing our mind helps us make the shift. For example, when we return from work, we should mentally put away our thoughts about unfinished projects, so as to be present for the other parts of our life.

This process of emptying is not to be confused with the escapism that comes from watching television or relaxing or chatting with friends. What I'm talking about is very different. It is non-doing, but with a purpose. It can take the form of reflection, meditation, or exercise. Like many people, I find jogging effective. When I jog, my attention is on nothing in particular. I focus on my breathing and the scenery. When new ideas pop into my head, I observe them and let them go.

Our breath can serve as "a convenient first object of attention to bring us back into the present moment," says Jon Kabat-Zinn, Professor of Medicine at the University of Massachusetts Medical School and founder of the Mindfulness-Based Stress Reduction Program. When we focus on our breathing, we are connecting to the present. "The last breath is gone, the next one hasn't come yet – it is always a matter of this one."[34] Being in the moment – connecting to who you're with and what you're doing – calls for improvisation as life unfolds. It also calls for taking everything as a continual lesson and allowing room for mistakes.

Prepare so you can relax. In 1982, Ang Peng Siong was the world's fastest 50m swimmer. When he was asked how he felt standing on the platform waiting for the starting horn in the race of his lifetime, he replied, "Relaxed." He had done all the work in the thousands of hours of training before that. There was nothing more to do except "be" in every second of the race.

Anyone who excels in music, performance, craft and so on knows that mastering a skill requires putting in hours of preparation. When a person gains competence, anxiety diminishes and he or she can focus on the moment. We need to prepare and

practise rigorously to perform with ease. Psychologist Mihaly Csikszentmihalyi, who famously came up with the term "flow", found that if a challenge is too great, people will be anxious. If a challenge is too simple, they may be bored. Feeling competent in a task gives us confidence to let go and "be"[35]. So put in the time needed to learn new skills. Prepare well so you can relax later.

OVER TO YOU

Cultivate the Clearing Habit

We're all different, but there are a variety of activities that can help us develop skills in being. Below is a list of suggested activities. Check those that work for you.

- ☐ Breathing
- ☐ Meditation
- ☐ Journaling
- ☐ Walking in nature
- ☐ Exercising
- ☐ Music
- ☐ Hobbies
- ☐ Reflecting
- ☐ Others:

Consider when was the last time you spent time on these activities? When is the next time you will do these again?

Go to www.wholenessinadisruptiveworld.com to listen to a guided breathing exercise to clear your mind.

Clearing in Stressful Situations

There are times we need to clear ourselves on the spot, e.g., in conflict situations, in meetings or when we feel fragmented. In these situations, I find it helpful to ask myself three questions:

1. **Mind:** What am I thinking? What are the different thoughts on my mind now?

2. **Heart**: How am I feeling? What are the different emotions?

3. **Body:** What are the different sensations in my body? What is my body telling me?

Notice that these questions point to the different parts within ourselves, as we commonly have thoughts mixed up with our feelings and bodily sensations. Acknowledging the different parts gives us awareness and choice. Now with this awareness, go back to your anchor. "What do you really want in this situation? What is aligned to your anchor?" Then take three deep breaths and do what is needed.

CHAPTER 7
INTEGRATING THE ABCs IN A DISRUPTIVE WORLD

"Each of us knows some part of the secret.
Each of us holds our small portion of the light.
We can thrive on earth only if we each bring
what we have and offer it at the family table."

– Wayne Mueller

We know that the magnitude, nature and frequency of change has shifted all around us. Technology, a game-changer, shortens business cycles and disrupts long-established routines and structures. Organisations continually restructure, resize and restrategise to survive. Planning horizons are shorter, strategy implementation has less lead time and people are repeatedly asked to do more with less. As a society, wider access to technology also means we all have avenues to express ideas, including extremist ideas, leading to more fragmentation of the community. We see increasing polarisation in the world, from terrorism and anti-globalisation movements to anti-immigrant sentiments.

At the individual level, the speed and sheer volume of information flows put unprecedented cognitive demands on us. We are chained to our gadgets 24/7, clearing emails and engaging in social media, fragmenting our attention and energy in the process. At work, we have more surprises and less control over our work as we face nagging uncertainty about how technological disruptions, like automation, artificial intelligence, big data or the internet of things, could affect our livelihood in the long term.

Alphabet Inc. executive chairman Eric Schmidt once said, "Our landscape has changed, yes, but our humanity will always remain, and that, above all else, is what makes us who we are."[36]

> *"How wonderful that we have met with a paradox. Now we have some hope of making progress."*
>
> **– Niels Bohr**

The ABCs of wholeness offer some ideas on how we can be "human" in this disruptive world.

WHOLENESS IN INDIVIDUALS AND LEADERS

Our individual wholeness is a necessary precursor to a productive and fulfilling life, not just for ourselves, but also for our families and communities.

Anchoring. The risk of not anchoring ourselves is to be swept along by currents of change, losing our focus, strength and sense of control. When we don't anchor, we disconnect from the core of who we are. Take time out to reflect on who you are as an individual and who you are in relation to your community. Our relationship with ourselves and our relationship with the world around us are both important. Only with a strong "I" can we serve the "We", and similarly, a healthy "We" supports us individually. So consider what are your values, purpose, identity and responsibilities?

Use the questions on page 107 to guide you. Talk to someone you trust. Write it down in a journal. It's okay if you don't have the complete answer. But start the process. In a workshop in Melbourne, a participant reflected, "I am struck by how I don't know my answers to these questions. It has never occurred to me to ask myself." If you have answers to these questions, periodically review them, because they can change as our life circumstances change.

Many organisations have personal leadership or leadership programmes that have a component on anchoring. I suggest adding these as part of the recruitment and onboarding process. This will identify the right fit for your organisation. Managers can also ask their staff these questions and share their own answers with them. This builds trust and engages every staff member as a full human being in their work, more than being merely a brain or a pair of hands.

Balancing. With clarity about our anchor, we expand our thinking and options. Is our solution based on either-or thinking or 50:50 compromise? Either-or solutions polarise and divide. Holistic solutions are 100:100 over the course of time. We want both "I" and "we" to win. We want fulfilment from our career as well as personal life. We want to bring both our mind and heart to work. We want to increase profits and take care of people. We want the benefits of technology and to take care of those who might be left behind. Balancing the opposing forces helps us to be creative. Be comfortable with the inherent tension and remove unnecessary limitations, including our past frameworks and models.

So examine your thinking and seek ways to integrate both opposing forces over time. The simple way of expressing this is to give and take. We may not have everyone win at the same time, but if we care for the larger whole, we allow the other side to gain now and know that our needs will be met in due time as well.

Use the tool on page 133 to balance your thinking. Do the exercise on a specific dilemma with your team or stakeholders. Working with an unbiased facilitator could be useful. This could be your human resources, strategic planning or organisation development staff, or anyone who has facilitation skills and is comfortable challenging the assumptions of the team. The less content expertise the facilitator has, the better. In fact, have your child ask you these questions!

Clearing. Take time to empty out and just "be". Just as sleep rejuvenates the body physically, emptying out rejuvenates the mind. How you connect with your team and what you say (and not say) can engage or disengage them. Are you aware of the needs of your team? Can they come to you to bounce ideas and get your full attention, or would you be half thinking about something else? Would your colleagues say you are calm and insightful when the ground is shifting under your feet?

When clearing and emptying out becomes an everyday practice, you can better access a calmer and wiser state of mind in times of chaos and change. So rather than feel like you're spinning around in a washing machine, you access the calm in the eye of the hurricane, and connect to who, when and what matters.

So step back from the constant doing. And I don't mean wait till your annual vacation to do this. That's too long a wait. Do it every day at a specific time of the day, early in the morning, during your lunch break or in the evening on the way home from work. I start my day with jogging, *taiji* or meditation. What about you? What works for you? Page 156 has a list of suggested activities – find what works for you and cultivate it as a habit.

In addition to the routine daily clearing, sometimes you may need to clear in the moment, especially in high-tension situations. Take note of strong emotions or bodily sensations in challenging situations as cues to clear judgments, negative emotions or ego. Access your anchor and balance your thinking to find more productive ways forward. These could be apologising, reprioritising or initiating a conversation with stakeholders.

As clearing is very much an individual internal practice, we can't make clearing a "standard operating procedure" or ask people to *just do it* in organisations. However, we can help increase people's awareness and skill in this. Lunchtime talks on this topic, role modelling by leaders and encouraging a few colleagues to come together to practice meditation after lunch are simple ways to get started. Where possible, designate private space for staff to have some quiet moments, e.g., meeting rooms that are not in use at lunchtime.

These ABCs of wholeness help us to be our best and do our best in our work and life over the long run. Here's a summary of the action ideas:

1. Clarify your own anchor.
2. Share your anchor with your team and ask them to share their anchors with you.
3. Use the Mobius Insight™ Tool to examine a dilemma.
4. Talk it through with a neutral party to test your thinking.
5. Cultivate a daily "clearing" activity.
6. Remind yourself when you need to "be" vs. "do" at work.

Based on these ideas, what might you advise Alan, the over-worked leader on the constant treadmill, to do? What about

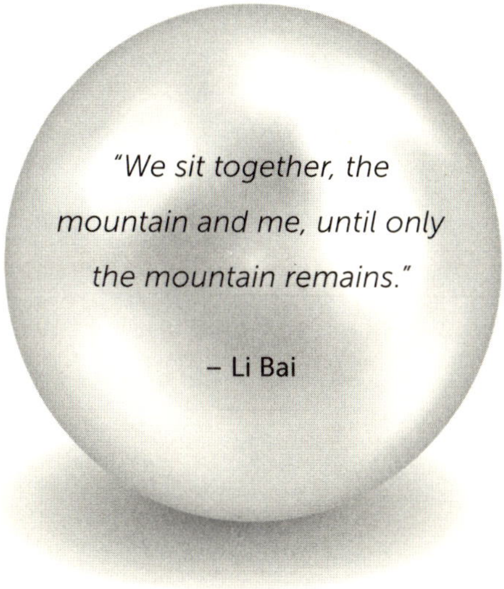

Maggie, the upcoming managing director who is torn by conflicting commitments in her career and family? What about Dave, the American integration manager operating in Asia? These are composite stories of real people captured in Chapter 2.

WHOLENESS IN ORGANISATIONS

Throughout the book, in addition to presenting individual stories as examples of wholeness, I have also woven in examples of organisations following the ABCs of wholeness. In other words, both individuals and organisations can be whole. Here are two more powerful examples.

GovTech and Hive. Officially launched in October 2015, Hive is an innovation hub under the Government Technology Agency of Singapore (GovTech) that comprises 100 specialists in data science, design, engineering and software development who come together to solve problems through innovative solutions[37]. Hive was originally formed under the Infocomm Development Authority (IDA), which underwent a major restructuring in 2016 and emerged as GovTech.

What is unique about Hive? It is managed separately from its parent organisation, and is housed in a separate building modelled after the Sandcrawlers from Star Wars. Instead of a typical hierarchy, Hive is organised in squads based on projects and relevant skills. Rather than typical performance appraisals, Hive relies on clear performance objectives and frequent

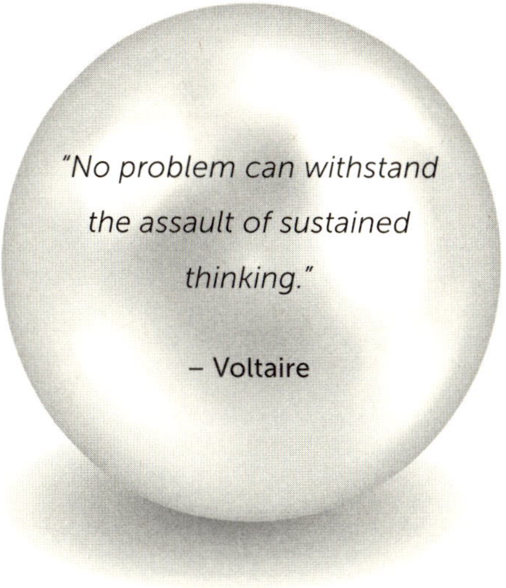

conversations to give feedback and assess performance. Instead of following a sequential process and rigid protocols – which is slower, higher-cost and liable to early obsolescence given the speed of change – Hive uses Agile methodology, which allows for changes on the fly. These specialists collaborate more closely, leading to faster, more useful and more relevant solutions.[38]

The results speak for themselves, with several successful apps having been developed for citizen use, such as MyResponder, where volunteers are notified of cardiac arrest cases within 400 metres of their location so someone can quickly perform CPR or apply the AED before an ambulance arrives. One of the experimental prototypes that Hive is creating uses a drone to inspect repairs needed in old factories. This approach is four times cheaper than manual site surveys[39].

Why is Hive managed so differently from GovTech, or for that matter, from the rest of the government? After all, accountability and transparency in the use of taxpayers' money remain a primary concern.

One possible answer is that the GovTech leadership understands the need for polarities to co-exist and is flexible in managing differently based on context. Given Hive's mission for speedy innovation, it has to experiment, be agile and allow space for failure (and fast failure). Within this, there is tension with the larger GovTech – rule-following vs. innovation, prudence vs. risk-taking, stability vs. change, slow vs. fast. Polarities co-exist here.

To succeed, Hive requires a different mindset, talent and management structure from the more traditional bureaucratic setup. With the clarity of its mission (anchor), GovTech takes a holistic view of how the organisation can be organised. The

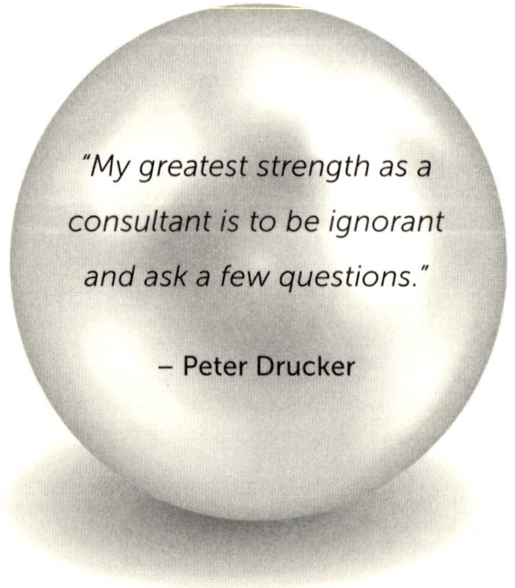

collaborative circular structures in Hive co-exist within the hierarchical triangular structure of the main GovTech organisation.

This flexibility is akin to water, which takes the shape of its container and can flow or be still. It can be gentle like a stream or forceful like crashing waves. So like water, Hive may change its form in future, but its mission continues to guide its evolution in the ever-changing environment. Emptying itself of prescribed forms leads to higher capacity to adapt and navigate tension, which in itself is a sign of life.

Berrett-Koehler (BK). BK is another example of a whole organisation. An independent publisher, its mission is to connect people and ideas to create a world that works for all. BK was founded in 1991 by Steve Piersanti, who had been fired from another major publishing house when he refused to comply with a directive from headquarters to cut headcount by 10 percent. According to Steve, "there was no rhyme or reason to do this, the company had a record-breaking year with 22 percent increase in sales and 46 percent increase in profits."[40] This defiance came at a personal cost to Steve, but it opened another opportunity. In the days after he lost his job, he received phonecalls from authors who gave him their manuscripts. Suppliers offered him much of the infrastructure for a publishing house on credit. No black-and-white contracts, just relationships and support to do what was right.

Today, the publishing business is being shaken up with self-publishing becoming a respectable and cost-efficient option, global distribution via channels like Amazon and Bookbaby, and ease of payment across the globe. Authors don't necessarily need publishers in the same way as the past. Fewer people read books as younger generations turn to videos and games for entertainment, and Google and Slideshare for information. Major bookstores are closing down. How does BK remain viable?

Today, BK publishes between 35 and 45 books a year, with a good number selling well. BK's success may be attributed to its wholeness. In Steve's foreword to the book *Stewardship* by Peter Block, he says, "Stewardship is one word to describe our mission – this is a deep sense of responsibility to administer the publishing company for the benefit of all 'stakeholder' groups – authors, customers, employees, suppliers and subcontractors, owners and societal and environmental communities in which we live and work."[41] It has a unique value proposition with books on progressive ideas and practices, a supportive "author with publisher" community and top-notch creative and marketing creations. In its management practices, BK seeks to avoid a "class system" by having one compensation system and banishing secrecy so employees know each other's pay and contribution, as well as company revenue and expenses.

Walking into BK's office in Oakland, I am greeted by Anders, Chief of First Impressions. Out of curiosity, I ask him, "You have an interesting job title. What do you do?" Flashing a wide smile, he explains, "Instead of calling it an admin role, my role is to welcome people, take care of the office and create a positive impression, since we only have one chance to get it right."

Wow, how many receptionists take their role so seriously and graciously?

As I walk around the neat, airy office, a friendly voice calls from behind me, "Has anyone shown you around yet?" Turning around, I meet Ginger, HR Director, a long-haired blonde. She has been at BK for more than 20 years. "What keeps you in BK for so long?" I ask, half surprised and half curious. "I can say what I really think here," comes the honest reply. This is a place where employees are treated as partners and their opinions are sought and valued.

BK says their work is to "help create a world that balances the needs of the person with the needs of the whole and believes that all of us can help us get there, one book at a time".[42] So with an investigative lens, I ask Ginger how the company does that. She shares an example of how the company handled the situation of younger staff wanting more leave.

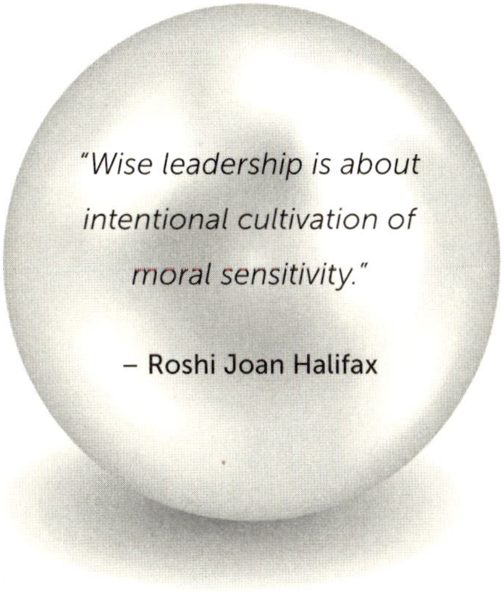

> *"He who attends to his greater self becomes a great man, and he who attends to his smaller self becomes a small man."*
>
> **– Mencius**

"Instead of simply following policies or judging younger staff for asking for something they do not deserve (yet)," Ginger says, "Steve suggested having a conversation to understand what people really wanted. After listening to both sides, we came up with an idea to meet both employees' and the company's needs." The solution was to designate the period between Christmas and New Year as holidays; this normally quiet period made the practice not a liability to the company. "It's not a perfect solution," Ginger says, "but the process got both sides to listen and understand one another." Within this approach is a balance of power and honouring one another as partners to find solutions together.

BK has both idealism and pragmatism, individual and community, business and relationships. It has had low employee turnover during its 24 years of operation, except for retirements. It is also the first publisher to be both a B Corp and Benefit

Corporation, which together are the gold standard for socially responsible businesses. Its financial results are well above publishing industry norms, with 9.9 percent increase in revenue in 2015. This shows that a whole organisation is also a healthy one.

OVER TO YOU

Wholeness in Your Life

Now it's over to you again. What key ideas struck a chord with you? Which of the ABCs – anchoring, balancing and clearing – is most relevant to you? What ideas can you use in your life? What are three things you can apply as a result of reading this book?

Wholeness in Organisations

You can also use these ABCs in the context of your organisation.

1. **Anchoring.** What anchors your organisation? What is its purpose, its values and responsibility? How do the stakeholders perceive the organisation?

2. **Balancing.** What is the polarity your organisation is dealing with, that if resolved, will move it forward?

3. **Clearing.** What does your organisation need to clear or let go of to reinvent itself in these disruptive times?

Or perhaps you have questions? You're welcome to share your thoughts and questions by joining the Wholeness Community on LinkedIn.[43]

EPILOGUE
WHOLENESS BEYOND "I"

"The parts can never be well unless the whole is well."

– Plato

As I dropped my six-year-old daughter, Sophie, at kindergarten one morning, she commanded me, "Sign this." It was a picture of a shark with characteristic razor-sharp teeth, and the words, "Say No to Shark Fin!" It already had some signatures on it, most of them her classmates'. It was a pledge to stop eating sharks fin soup, a common delicacy in Chinese culture. Sophie described the cruel practice of throwing the sharks back into the sea only for them to drown without their fins. I signed it, and I have kept my word.

On another occasion, in the car on the way home from school, Sophie declared, "We must not use air-conditioning because the holes in the ozone layer will get bigger." I was impressed by what she had been learning in school. Then I realised the implications of sweltering 30-plus Celsius (90-plus Fahrenheit) afternoons. Sophie is an example of the next generation living into the future, the one we will leave for them.

How is this related to wholeness? Wholeness is not just individual. Wholeness is also the community. The *Dao De Jing* describes it this way:

> *He who values the world as himself*
> *May then be entrusted with the government of the world;*
> *And he who loves the world as himself,*
> *The world may then be entrusted to his care.*

Individual and collective wholeness are intertwined. Whole individuals develop the capacity to contribute to something larger than themselves. When the larger whole is healthy, it in turn supports the well-being of the individual. This is like healthy leaves of a tree contributing to a larger healthy tree. Individually healthy trees contribute to a thriving forest. We see the community as integral to us instead of separate from us. This community could be our family, team, organisation, local community, country, the environment, or the entire planet.

Khoo Boon Hui

Boon Hui is an example of an individual serving the collective wholeness. The police commissioner of Singapore from 1997 to 2010 and president of INTERPOL from 2008 to 2012, he

describes his perspective this way: "Wholeness is seeing yourself and the organisation in service to a higher purpose, whether nationally or globally. We open our minds to greater possibilities when we contribute."

Living by this philosophy as the police commissioner, he instituted the slogan "A Force for the Nation", which became an enduring vision that guides the men and women of the Singapore Police Force (SPF).[44] This vision deepened citizen-centred policing with an emphasis on building trust between police and community. This goes beyond traditional enforcement work. "When an organisation's mission is defined too narrowly, it loses attention on the interests of the collective whole," says Boon Hui in a gentle tone.

His desire to contribute to the community was tested during the Al-Qaeda terrorist attacks. As a member of the administrative

service of the Singapore civil service, Boon Hui was under consideration for a new post when the 9/11 attack brought down the World Trade Center towers in New York. Soon after, Bali was bombed by extremist group Jemaah Islamiyah. As the threat of terrorism escalated in the region, Boon Hui decided not to leave the police force. A steadying hand was needed to help the SPF fulfil its mission during this turbulent period.

This decision meant that he missed an opportunity to be posted to another area of public service, which would have been the expected career path for an administrative officer (the leadership cadre of the Singapore civil service). When asked whether he regrets the decision, he looks into the distance and replies, "One should make decisions based on one's inner purpose. I ask myself, 'What more can I do?' And I contribute wherever I am." With this as his anchor, Boon Hui took the path less travelled, which eventually saw him serve as police commissioner for another eight years. In the course of his police career, Boon Hui took pride in developing other leaders, who have gone on to make great contributions of their own.

Boon Hui also served the international community through INTERPOL. Why would the tiny island of Singapore bother policing internationally when Singapore's crime rates are among the lowest in the world? In response, Boon Hui says, "We may be small, but we have a long tradition of collaboration with other police forces around the world." This provides an example of contributing in a wider way.

International cooperation with foreign law enforcement, which is one of the key tenets behind INTERPOL, combats the challenges posed when criminals and terrorists exploit globalisation and technology. The SPF has therefore become a strong supporter of INTERPOL and its activities. For example, it hosts the INTERPOL Global Complex for Innovation, which attracts expertise from both the public and private sectors worldwide to work together on current and future crime concerns. In today's context of an open, globalised environment, such international police cooperation is critical to help Singapore combat international and organised crime. In addition, the nation will enhance its position on the international stage as a recognised centre of excellence in safety and security.

INTEGRATING "I" AND "WE"

Dr. Daniel J. Siegel, a professor of clinical psychiatry at the UCLA School of Medicine and author of *The Developing Mind: How Relationships and the Brain Interact to Shape Who We Are*[45], coined the word "mwe" by combining "me" and "we". This is an elegant integration, creating language for individual and collective wholeness. He explains, "To be wise leaders, we need to have insight about ourselves, personal emotional balance, concern and empathy for others, and a sense of interconnectedness with the world." This integration has a neurobiological correlate. Dr. Siegel's research shows that when we pay attention, the synapses in our brains increase and develop more cross connections. Linking these different parts then helps us better regulate our behaviour.[46]

I want to offer a framework that unites "I" and "We". This is adapted from the work of Dr. David Hawkins, a psychiatrist,

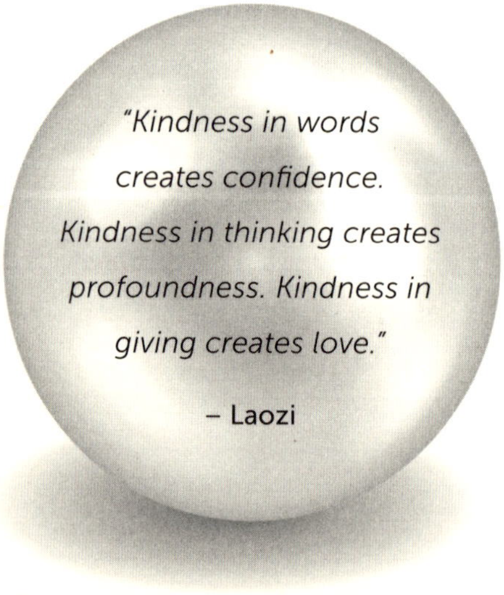

researcher and spiritual teacher who developed a rubric for the levels of human consciousness by using behavioural kinesiology. The statements and perspectives he developed reflect levels of energy. I have simplified these levels in an "I to We" Framework:

Levels

We	**Empathy:** I care for the larger world and know I am connected with you, even if we are strangers.
	Love: I care for people in my smaller circle of community, e.g., family and close friends.
	Accountability: I am responsible for myself and my world.
I/We	**Curiosity:** I like to try and create new things.
I	**Pride and Desire:** I take pride in my work and want to be regarded positively.
	Self-Protection: I need to protect my interests in a threatening world.
	Apathy: I don't know, I don't see and I don't care.

Integrating "I" and "We" means we treat the world as if it is our own because the larger whole is part of us. This means to love a stranger or someone else's child. With empathy (the highest level), we experience the world from another person's perspective and feel a connection with him or her. Empathy leads to loving kindness, making contribution to the larger community a natural outcome. We also see that through our actions and non-actions, we contribute to the world around us.

BALANCING "I" AND "WE"

My mentor Peter once asked my father what his dream was. Peter posed the question over dinner with the entire family present plus some friends. My father laughed and shook his head, "I don't have dreams, I'm so old already." Peter, being the persistent consultant, asked again, "If you had a dream, what would it be?" My father mumbled something about wanting to be a sailor when he was a young lad. But he had been helping out in the family coffeeshop business since his teens. So that dream was extinguished. Peter asked the same question a few more times in various ways, and finally my father said, "To see the children grow up", referring at first to me and my siblings. As we are now grown up, he continued, "And now help out with the grandchildren." He is fulfilling his dream: to spend his entire life taking care of the family. For this, I am very grateful.

In Eastern cultures, responsibility weighs heavily, often squeezing out any notion of "I" or identity other than family. Being responsible is not a bad thing, but the risk is that responsibility takes over fully, leaving us disconnected from our freedom, passion and personal purpose. I am aware of and grateful for the sacrifices of the earlier generations, which have given us the means to develop "I".

Sheryl Sandberg, author of *Lean In*[47], wrote that women in particular need to shift their mindset from neglecting their personal goals to embracing self-care. In a study, she found that men and women who prioritised their own needs along with those of others achieve high performance and have low burnout. This approach might seem less altruistic than prioritising others' needs above the self, but individuals who adopt it gain influence and sustain their own energy to actually give more in the long run. Claire Chiang, co-founder of Banyan Tree Hotels & Resorts, whom you met in Chapter 2, lives this I/we integration. She pursues her aspirations and contributes to society. In her words, "a strong 'I' is needed for the good of 'we'".

Strolling in a San Francisco suburb, I saw that the houses were distinctive, with no two the same. This is very interesting as houses in Singapore typically have common designs, with an emphasis on practicality and cost over design. This "I" focus

gives space for personal aspirations, interests and creativity to flourish. I also admire the respect for individual rights and human dignity. There is constructive activism in putting forth one's opinions for the community.

In Eastern societies, we tend to have a core team of experts think through issues and a leadership team that makes decisions. Individuals are invited to contribute their ideas, but the process of hearing individual voices does not stop laws from being passed or unpopular policies from being implemented. This is perhaps why China and Singapore can move quickly, e.g., build infrastructure like train lines even though they disrupt the homes of some individuals, and yes, ban the sale of chewing gum in Singapore to keep the streets clean! The good of the larger whole is prioritised over individual rights.

URGENCY IN INTEGRATING "I" AND "WE"

We need to integrate "I" and "we" urgently for the benefit of both the individual and community. Flipping through the newspapers, we see climate change, refugees, terrorism, anti-globalisation, ageing populations, loneliness in the headlines. We witness horrific acts of terror committed in the name of anti-Western movements, triggering equally strong backlash and suspicion. The polarisation of the haves and have-nots divides countries.

In my neighbourhood, I see elderly women toiling under the hot sun for their livelihood. They spend the majority of their day collecting, transporting and selling cardboard for 10 to 12 cents

> *"It is not enough to win a war; it is more important to organise the peace."*
>
> – Aristotle

per kilo. They push a heavy trolley around, often hunched over and wearing the same patched-up clothes every day. Doing the maths, they earn $2 to $4 a day.

One day, I jogged past one of these women. She was trying to push her trolley up a series of steps. I stopped to help. A couple of Indian foreign workers stopped to help too. But she refused to receive our help, proud in her self-reliance. We didn't understand and, trying to be helpful, pushed her trolley up the steps anyway. Then she exclaimed in a local dialect, "Now you push my trolley away, how am I going to climb up?" At that moment, I realised her trolley was also her crutches. Embarrassed, we brought her trolley back down, she thanked us and insisted she would manage on her own. Not knowing how to help, I continued my jog. Now when I see her, we smile and greet each other. Sometimes, I offer her a packet of rice or noodles, as a little way of helping.

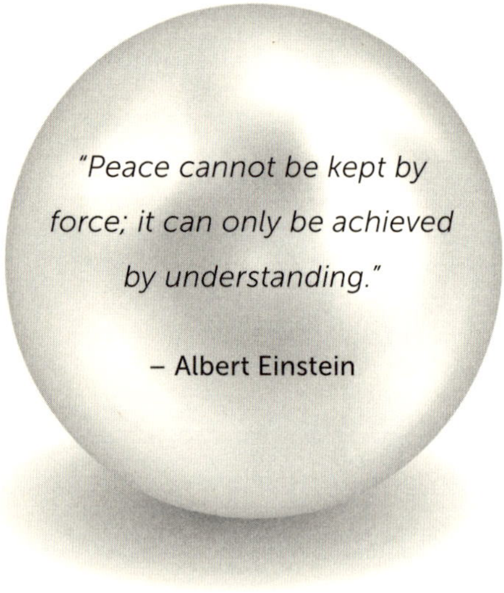

In the workplace, constant restructuring and right-sizing wears out our spirit at work. Rather than champion a project we believe in, we take a wait-and-see approach in case our efforts are wasted by a change in management directive. We put in long hours along with phone calls at night and long commutes to be responsible in the work. But responsibility is different from being fully alive and engaged. In my workshops, I ask participants to consider, can we be bothered to:

- Tell our boss that his idea won't work and we have a better one?

- Tell our customers a better way when they insist on their own?

- Improve or simplify a process that is cumbersome?

- Challenge our colleagues on their thinking?
- Go against policies because something else makes better sense?
- Try something new that has no guarantee of success?
- Advocate for a new idea that goes against the current norms?
- Tell a colleague his blind spot so he can improve?
- Ask our staff how they are doing in their work and life?
- Find out our colleagues' career aspirations and nurture them?

Typically I hear groans followed by knowing nods amongst the participants in response to these questions. We know what we are talking about and what we should do, but we also know it is easier to just "go along" and not make so much trouble (for ourselves and others), and tread the predictable path. It takes more effort and is riskier to "bother". After all, we are very busy tossing many balls in the air. To be engaged and alive in our work is to care about "I" and "We".

"WE" FOCUS CAN BE SIMPLE TOO

Caring for collective wholeness doesn't necessarily call for large sacrificial acts of contribution on the scale of Mother Teresa, Harry Truman, Nelson Mandela or Lee Kuan Yew. Small, simple acts of community involvement make a difference too.

Simple acts of kindness remind us of our common humanity. One evening, I took a taxi home from work, lost in my thoughts about an earlier meeting and my "to do" list for the next day. As the taxi came close to home, I discovered to my horror that I didn't have enough cash to pay the fare. The credit card machine wasn't working either. The Malay taxi driver said, "Never mind, you transfer the money to my account." Feeling grateful, I replied, "Okay, thank you. I will do it immediately when I get back." I was surprised to hear him reply, "Never mind, it's late already. You rest first and transfer when you have time. Anyway, money won't bring us to heaven."

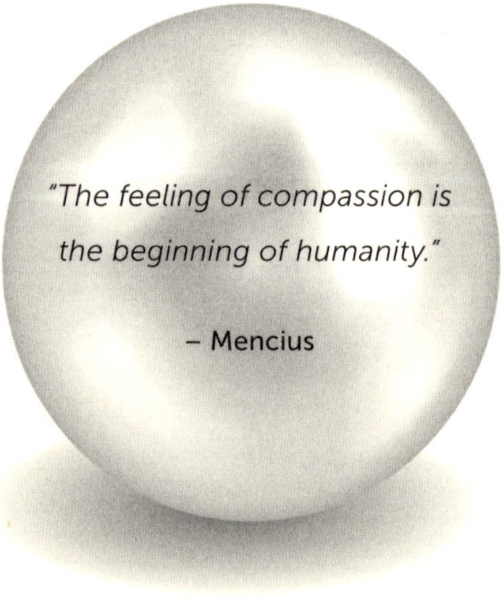

A simple and not-so-well-off man, he works more than 12 hours a day to make a living, yet he remains generous and trusting. I feel a sense of connection to and gratitude for people like him who remind me of the beauty of simplicity. This is a stark contrast to well-travelled and well-educated but generally distrusting, distant and distracted people.

Consider these actions:

- Drive considerately, giving way to others
- Say hello to fellow joggers
- Pick up litter
- Offer food to an elderly neighbour
- Share an umbrella with a stranger
- Give directions to tourists who seem lost
- Hold the elevator when someone is rushing to catch it
- Connect people for business and/or mutual learning

When we work toward community wholeness, we help others without expecting a return. This creates a sense of neighbourliness rather than perpetuating transactional exchange amongst strangers. We are more aware of others rather than oblivious to their needs. We build bridges instead of walls. We reach out instead of minding our own business. We include and welcome, rather than draw lines.

Buddha said that when our heart is as big as the ocean, a drop of ink disappears into it. But if our heart is as small as a bowl of water, the same drop of ink discolours it. We choose how big we allow our hearts to be. Can our hearts be as big as the community? Rather than separating and drawing lines between "This is me and that is you", it is an intentional choice to take the stand that "You are part of me".

The first time I felt a strong sense of togetherness with the larger Singapore community was when I was in the queue for four hours with my three children (aged nine, seven and four at the time) and hundreds of thousands of other Singaporeans to pay our last respects to Mr Lee Kuan Yew. At that time of year, the weather was hot and clammy, with rain constantly threatening. The queue snaked along the streets past a church, a hotel and a large field.

This gathering gave me a heartfelt sense of camaraderie with my fellow countrymen. We came together in our sadness and vulnerability. Amid the crowd and heat, fellow Singaporeans remained patient and helped one another. Strangers shared paper fans to move the stifling air and gave each other smiles and nods of acknowledgement. People around me made way for my stroller, occasionally cautioning one another with polite comments such as, "Wait, there is a small child here." They were also gracious when I accidentally pushed the stroller into their ankles. Once I had to cut the line and rush to the front, chasing

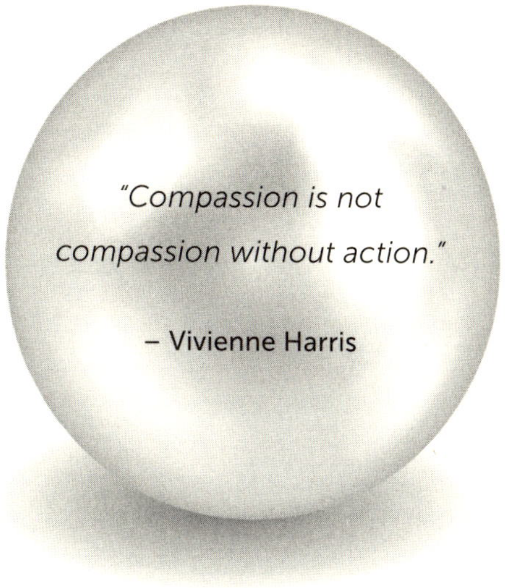

my boys who had raced ahead. Instead of the indignant disapproval people usually display when others cut in front of them, one man made way for me, saying, "I understand. I have children too."

Singaporeans have a reputation for being *kiasu* (fearful of losing). This sense of community with my countrymen was both touching and surprising. The death of our leader brought us together and revealed the gentle and compassionate side of humanity. And it showed me the beauty in pursuing a larger sense of wholeness.

Visiting the 9/11 memorial at Ground Zero in New York for the first time, I was struck by the anguish, terror and also the great sense of togetherness in Americans. A quote by an eyewitness on a black exhibit wall stood out: "While we still looked up, a man jumped from the building. White shirt, black pants, end-over-end tumbling to the ground. At that instant, the towering glass and metal mass of billowing smoke became human." In grief, we share our humanity. This experience galvanised Americans and much of the world. The best and worst of humanity came through in the aftermath of this incident, however, as the last inscription inspires hope: "We came in as individuals. And we'll walk out together."

So here's my invitation. Include "we" in your anchor. Be more aware of "we" than being preoccupied in our "I" world. Expand our thinking to take care of our needs and the needs of the wider community. These might sound idealistic, but it's certainly a possibility as we cultivate wholeness – yours, mine and ours.

Cultivated in the individual, character will become genuine;
Cultivated in the family, character will become abundant;
Cultivated in the village, character will multiply;
Cultivated in the state, character will prosper;
Cultivated in the world, character will become universal.
– *Dao De Jing*, Chapter 54

Thank you. 谢谢！

OVER TO YOU

You and Your World

Notice the world you live in – home, work, neighbourhood, community and even country. What would more wholeness in these worlds be like? How would it support the people involved or even you? What small actions can you contribute to create larger wholeness?

Share with us on the Wholeness Community LinkedIn page to keep your momentum going and inspire others to do the same!

"You must not lose faith in humanity. Humanity is an ocean; if a few drops of the ocean are dirty, the ocean does not become dirty."

– Mahatma Gandhi

PRACTICE BEYOND THE BOOK

I hope you have found the ideas and exercises in this book useful. It is time to apply them to live a life of wholeness. Integrating the ABCs of wholeness into everyday life requires committed practice. My intention is to support you, so I have developed an array of resources at Flame Centre. Do pick one or two and move forward.

Community. Rather than walk alone, join like-minded people to support and challenge one another. You make the community. Access it from the www.wholenessinadisruptiveworld.com website.

Keynotes. I am a Certified Professional Speaker (CSP), an international measure of professional platform competence, and I have a track record of presenting at conferences and organisations to inspire and educate.

Learning experiences. To go deeper into the content and apply these ideas in your work and life, consider the range of options available – online content, blended learning and face-to-face workshops, with exercises, tools and practices. You can access these options from the website. Solutions for organisations are available too.

Coaching. We all have our unique context and challenges. It helps to talk through things with someone. Engage a wholeness coach to explore how you can apply the ABCs of wholeness in a targeted way in your life.

Visit **www.wholenessinadisruptiveworld.com** for more information or scan this QR code to access it:

NOTES

1 Global Talent 2021. https://www.oxfordeconomics.com/Media/Default/Thought%20Leadership/global-talent-2021.pdf

2 Richard Foster. Yale University. http://www.bbc.com/news/business-16611040

3 Global Workforce Study. 2012. Towers Watson, http://www.towerswatson.com/assets/pdf/2012-Towers-Watson-Global-Workforce-Study.pdf

4 http://globenewswire.com/news-release/2013/04/09/536945/10027728/en/Workplace-Stress-on-the-Rise-With-83-of-Americans-Frazzled-by-Something-at-Work.html, accessed 18 Nov 2016.

5 Social Times Study. 2013. http://www.adweek.com/socialtimes/smartphones/480485

6 American Psychological Association. "Stress Survey: Stress a Major Health Problem in the U.S." APA Help Center. 2007. http://www.apahelpcentere.org/articles/article.php?id=165.

7 http://www.iftf.org/uploads/media/SR-1382A_UPRI_future_work_skills_sm.pdf

8 Self-reported work-related illness and workplace injuries in 2008/09: Results from the Labour Force Survey. 2010.

9 Gallup. State of American Workplace. 2013. http://www.gallup.com/strategicconsulting/163007/state-american-workplace.aspx

10 http://businessjournal.gallup.com/content/22720/worker-disengagement-continues-cost-singapore.aspx

11 https://business.linkedin.com/talent-solutions/blog/2014/01/top-10-job-titles-that-didnt-exist-5-years-ago-infographic

12 Richard E. Nisbett. *Geography of Thought: How Asians and Westerners Think Differently...and Why*. Free Press. 2004.

13 http://www.rcgd.isr.umich.edu/news/Nisbett&Oyserman.NewScientist_03.2009.pdf, accessed 9 Jan 2015

14 Parker Palmer, *A Hidden Wholeness: The Journey Toward An Undivided Life*. Wiley. 2009.

15 http://thinkbusiness.nus.edu/article/the-capitaland-approach-to-management/

16 https://www.challenge.gov.sg/print/letters-to-a-young-public-officer/bring-your-whole-self-to-public-service

17 http://www.straitstimes.com/sport/gold-for-yip-pin-xiu-at-rio-paralympics

18 http://youtu.be/35P28I3T7Po

19 Robin R. Wang. Yinyang: *The Way of Heaven and Earth in Chinese Thought and Culture* (*New Approaches to Asian History*). Cambridge University Press. 2012.

20 The Crack Up, 1945

21 http://www.english.illinois.edu/maps/poets/s_z/whitman/song.htm

22 Translated from *Tsun Tzu – Theory of Governance*

23 Robert Kaplan and Robert Kaiser. *Fear Your Strengths: What You Are Best at Could Be*. Berrett Koehler, 2013

24 Ibid.

25 https://www.mindtools.com/pages/article/newSTR_91.htm

26 http://en.wikipedia.org/wiki/Tao_Te_Ching

27 *The Geography of Thought*, published by Free Press, 2003

28 Kevin Cashman. *Leadership from the Inside Out: Becoming a Leader for Life*. Berrett-Koehler. 2nd Edition. 2008.

29 P. Goldberg. *The Intuitive Edge*. J.P. Tarcher. 1983.

30 https://hbr.org/2014/03/mindfulness-in-the-age-of-complexity/ar/1, accessed 8 March 2015

31 https://hbr.org/2014/03/mindfulness-in-the-age-of-complexity/ar/1, accessed 8 March 2015.

32 Ellen J. Langer. *Mindfulness in the Age of Complexity*. https://hbr.org/2014/03/mindfulness-in-the-age-of-complexity/ar/1, accessed 8 March 2015.

33 *Leading in Context*. Duke Corporate University. 2013.

34 *Mindfulness for Beginners*, 2006, Sounds True, Colorado

35 *Flow: The Psychology of Optimal Experience*, Harper Collins, 2008

36 http://news.berkeley.edu/2012/05/14/google-ceo-to-graduates-the-future-doesnt-just-happen/

37 https://www.ida.gov.sg/Tech-Scene-News/Tech-News/Digital-Government/2015/11/A-Hive-of-Digital-Dynamism

38 https://govinsider.asia/digital-gov/singapores-coolest-startup/

39 https://www.techinasia.com/ida-hive-govtech-singapore

40 https://www.bkconnection.com/blog/posts/how-berrett-koehler-began

41 https://www.bkconnection.com/static/Stewardship_2nd_EXCERPT.pdf

42 https://www.bkconnection.com/home/bk-community-menu/about-berrett-koehler-publishers?redirected=true

43 www.wholenessinadisruptiveworld.com

44 http://www.challenge.gov.sg/archives/2005_11/people/ppl06.html

45 Dr. Daniel J. Siegel. *The Developing Mind: How Relationships and the Brain Interact to Shape Who We Are*. The Guilford Press; Second Edition. 2015.

46 Wisdom 2.0 Conference, 18 and 19 June 2015, Singapore.

47 Random House, 2013

ACKNOWLEDGMENTS

I never thought I would be writing this page. I would like to express my heartfelt gratitude to the many people who have guided and encouraged me on this long journey:

To Peter Block, who challenged me to dig deeper and find my voice. Your question, "What's new?" haunted me for a long time and I was relieved when you finally said it's unique and interesting enough to warrant further action!

To Geoff Bellman, for being my first editorial coach and opening my eyes to better writing, and really being ever so responsive to my questions and guiding me into the complex world of publishing.

To Paul Wang, for being my Chinese teacher and sparking new insights in every conversation. The wisdom of Chinese thinking in this book is attributed to you.

To Andrew Matthews, for being a sounding board with your authentic and thoughtful thinking on wholeness. I learnt a lot from you and admire your spirit.

To Robin Speculand, who challenged and supported me beyond the call of your mentoring duty. Thanks for listening to my hesitation and stirring me to keep going.

To Bev Kaye, Pauline Arneberg, Maya Hu-Chan, Linda Tan, Lindley Craig, Joanna Flinn, Sarah Schubert, Andrea Edwards and Ron Kaufman, for cheering me on, guiding me and giving me feedback on earlier versions of the book.

To Laura Schenone and Herb Schaffner, for your masterful developmental editorial support that lifted the strengths of the book to what it is now.

To Melvin Neo, Justin Lau, and all at Marshall Cavendish, for believing in a first-time author and taking pride in doing good work, which made our collaboration so fruitful.

To KY, for tending to the kids while I escaped many nights to write, for being an honest critic and most of all, for supporting and loving me despite my occasional un-whole ways.

ACKNOWLEDGMENTS

To all the leaders I interviewed and learnt from – Lim Boon Huat, Claire Chiang, Lau Yin Cheng, Tan Kay Yong, David Chang, Susan Chong, Khoo Boon Hui, Ang Peng Siong, Ong Boon Kee and Aaron Maniam – this book would not have been possible without your wisdom.

ABOUT THE AUTHOR

Wendy Siew-Inn Tan is an explorer at heart. Led by curiosity and care, her work is about learning and bringing forth ideas to help us act with wisdom for the greater good. Being a Chinese with a Western education, Wendy draws from both wells to find insight and inspiration for us to be better human beings.

Wendy co-founded Flame Centre in 2004, a talent development and instructional design practice based in Asia. Flame Centre's work in integrating pedagogy and technology for learning advantage recently won the InnovPlus Spark and HRO Today Thought Leadership Awards.

Wendy is a Certified Professional Speaker (CSP), a designation conferred by the National Speakers Association as the international measure of professional platform competence. Wendy

has conducted keynotes and presented widely in conferences and organisations. She connects with her audience through her authentic, heartful and thought-provoking disposition.

As a consultant and facilitator, Wendy enjoys partnering with clients to bring about an alternative future where people and businesses thrive. Flame Centre also represents the work of Dr Beverly Kaye in career development and talent engagement solutions and Peter Block's Flawless Consulting workshops in the Asia Pacific region. Wendy has worked with many multinational corporations and government agencies in her career.

Wendy holds a Masters of Science in Organization Development (MSOD) from Pepperdine University and graduated from the National University of Singapore in Psychology with honours. She is based in Singapore with her husband Kang Yam and three children, Pete, Finn and Sophie.

Email Wendy at **Wendy_Tan@flamecentre.com** or connect with her on LinkedIn at **sg.linkedin.com/in/wendy-flame**.